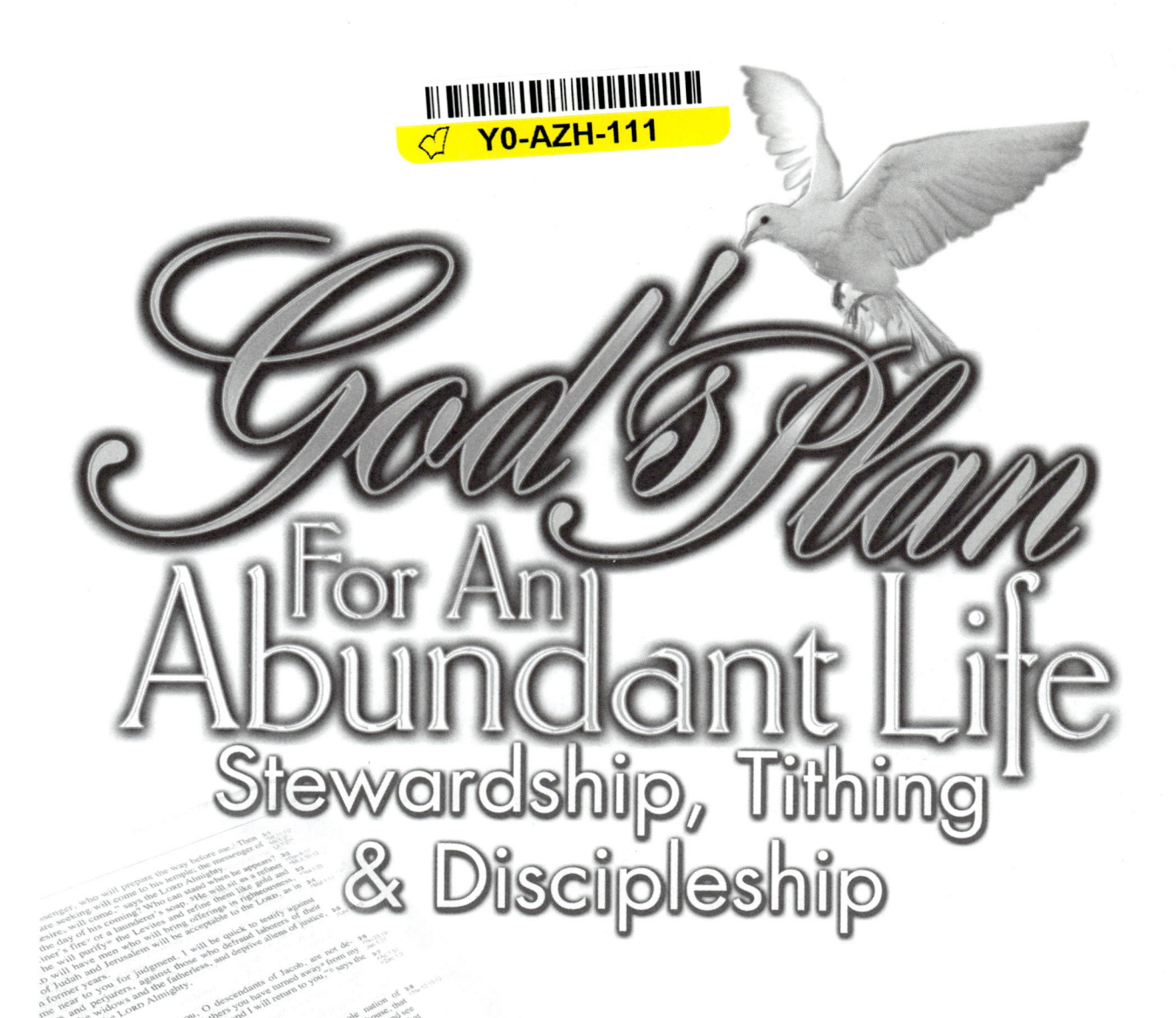

God's Plan For An Abundant Life
Stewardship, Tithing & Discipleship

Written by: Anton L. Seals, Sr.
Chief Editor: Wasi Young, Executive Director Umoja People, *African Centered Programs*
Editorial Assistants: A. Maxine Seals, Rev. Richard Posey
Cover and Text Design: Michelle D. Muhammad, MDM Design
Published by: VASTT Ministry, Inc.
Revised Edition
Second Printing
ISBN: 0-9759644-0-2

© TXU1-049-878 2002 VASTT Ministry, Inc.

All rights reserved. No part of this publication may be reproduced, stored in a retrieval system, or transmitted in any form or by means, electronic, mechanical, photocopy, recording or otherwise except for brief quotations in printed reviews without prior written permission from the holder of the copyright. Printed in the United States of America.

GOD'S PLAN FOR AN ABUNDANT LIFE: Stewardship, Tithing & Discipleship

This Book Is In Memory Of:

I must acknowledge the precious memories of loving family members who have gone on to be with our Lord: especially my Mama, (Allegra). It was her mothers love, determination, generosity and faith in God to endure, that shaped the foundation of who I am today. She expected nothing but the best for us. Also, my loving brother Walter, who pulled me up when I was down, my deceased wife, Velveteen, who taught me the meaning of unconditional Love. Pops and Granny, (Lawrence & Estelle Townzel), who taught me to fear and trust in God. They lived a life pleasing to God. To my loving and caring Auntie Yvonne Anderson, who lived next door to us for many years: for her prayers, love and support. To my father, Walter, and stepmother, Mother Ida, who encouraged me to remain in the ministry.

To my Great Grand father, Rev. Lawrence Townzel, Sr. who I never knew. I have his Bible and the notes from the late 1800's and early 1900's. The seed of Abraham has been passed on to another generation, and for every generation to come. May the seed, of the seed, be blessed of God and may every child become a servant for the Lord and seek His righteousness

In memory of Frank Parker (1984 - 2004)

Frank's tragic and sudden death is an awakening of the evil that prevails on the minority youth across America; particularly urban black and Hispanic youth. Frank is not a statistic, he was a young man who loved life and came from a loving and caring mother and family. It is my prayer for my son Aaron and the children of Sister Gayle Parker; mother; and all the children of God, that we will not allow Frank's life to have been be in vain. Please, brothers and sisters STOP the KILLING!

GOD'S PLAN FOR AN ABUNDANT LIFE: Stewardship, Tithing & Discipleship

Table Of Contents

In Memory Of 3

Dedication 6

Endorsements 7-8

Introduction 9-10

Seminar 1

Stewardship Characteristics: Stewards Are God's Anointed Managers 11

Outline of Seminar 1 12
A Plan For An Abundant Life 13
Purpose of The Manual 14
Defining Stewards 15-19
What Kind of Seward Are You? 20-21
God's Plan for Stewardship 22-23
Stewards Have A Fruitful Inheritance 24-31
Stewards Are Not Jealous and Selfish 32-33
Stewards Are Accountable: 34-35
Stewards Serve God and Manage Wealth Wisely 36
Stewards Have Power To Get Wealth 36-37
Stewards Lay There Treasures In Heaven 37
Stewards Seek The Righteousness of God 37
Stewards Willingly Give 38
Stewards Are Faithful and Know How To Pray 38-39
Stewards Are Not Hypocrites 39
Stewards Are Faithful of The Talents 40-41
Stewards Are Entrusted With God's Mysteries 42
Stewards Know When and How To Collect 43-44
Stewards Are Not Greedy 44
Stewards Have Strength and Are Content 44
Steward Are Filled With Grace 45
Stewards Provide for The Church 46
Stewards Know How To Sow and Give Willingly 46-47
Stewards Are Not Deceitful 48
Stewards Are Transformed 48

3

GOD'S PLAN FOR AN ABUNDANT LIFE: Stewardship, Tithing & Discipleship

Table Of Contents

Seminar 2

Worship God By Giving Your Tithes & Offerings — **51**
Outline of Seminar 2 — 52
Introduction, Purpose & Mission — 53-54
Managing God's Wealth — 55
God's Way Versus Our Ways — 56
Historical Relationship of Tithing — 57
Tithing History — 58-62

Group Activity I: (1-9): What God Said About Tithing — 63-71

Group Activity II:
    The Three T's — 72
    Bible Truths — 73
R U Factors — 74
Tithes and Offerings (A Covenant Commitment With God) — 75-76
Key Factors That Help To Develop A Life of Tithing — 77-78

Group Activity III:
    God's Plan for A Spirit Filled Life: (Stewardship & Discipleship) — 79-85
    It Is Not What It Looks Like: Believe and Operate In Faith — 86-87
    Principles of Giving — 87
    Why The Church Must Teach Giving — 88
Why Give To God? — 91
Difference Between Fund-Raisers & Tithing — 91-92
God Wants Your Best Sacrificial Offering — 92
Giving Your Tithes and Offering — 93-94
Sowing and Reaping Your Abundant Harvest — 95-99
How Can The People Hear Without A Pastor? — 100-101
You Must Trust God and The God In Your Pastor — 102-103
Giving With A Willing Heart — 104-110

GOD'S PLAN FOR AN ABUNDANT LIFE: Stewardship, Tithing & Discipleship

Table Of Contents

Seminar 3

Discipleship: A Foundation For Tithing & Stewardship	**112**
Outline of Seminar 3	113
Introduction	114-116
What Is Discipleship	117-121
Disciples Have A Paradigm Shift In Their Thinking	122-123
Group Exercise On Discipleship Principles	**124**
Treasure Chest of Knowledge John 17:1-26	125
Christian Discipleship & Leadership Characteristic	126

John 17:1		Disciples Lift Up The Name of Jesus	126
	V2	Disciples Have Power and Authority	126
	V3	Disciples Have New Life	127
	V4	Disciples Finish The Work	127
	V5	Disciples Know God As The Alpha & Omega	128
	V6	Disciples Teach & Live According To God' Word	128
	V7-26	(Go to Page 129)	129

Disciples Love The Lord & Their Neighbors	130
Disciples Are Made Not Born	132
Study and Know the Truth	132-133
Prerequisites For Becoming A Disciple	133-135
Discipleship Group Exercise	**136**
A Briefing For The Case Study	136-137
Your Group Challenge	138
Your Mission	138-140
Discipleship Group Exercise	**141**
Instructions No Greater Joy Than Knowing The Truth	141
No Greater Joy Than Knowing The Truth	141
Twelve Principles of Discipleship	142
A Life of Discipleship & Stewardship 100% Tithers	143

GOD'S PLAN FOR AN ABUNDANT LIFE: Stewardship, Tithing & Discipleship

This Book Is Dedicated To:
My Loving Family and Friends:

To My wife Maxine: a loving and caring woman of God. Thank you for trusting God and supporting VASTT Ministry as I have devoted my life to the things of God. Your sacrifices have gone up as a memorial before God and I believe I hear God saying Stand still and see the Salvation of the Lord. May God richly bless you and the vision you have and for sticking by me.

To My Sons: Anton Jr., Shamon and Aaron, and your mother Sharon, my first wife, each of you are special gifts from God. I thank God for your thoughtful and compassionate ways for caring and you have made us proud parents. I am blessed to be your father and dad/daddy/pop. To Alfonso, Tallie and Verlene: I thank God for your mother Velveteen, who we know is looking down from heaven. Through it all you have stayed the course. Your faith has kept you going and you are truly blessed. I am so very proud you, too. To Sons and Daughters: Angelo, Anthony and Alexis and Kristin: When I married your mother, (Maxine) I also took on the responsibility of building a strong relationship with each of you. You have made it easy, thank you for opening your hearts to me and for being honest. Kristin is my forever innocent and strong-minded child. You are truly blessed and thanks for the love.

To Papa Joe for unwavering love and support. Thanks you for the wisdom, and especially for listening to me when things seem impossible to bare. Your faith and love is so precious, thanks for your unconditional love of my Mom. To Bernard and my praying Sister In-law Linda, God bless you for helping me through those difficult days. Your Latter Rain experiences begin now. My Aunt Rheta and Uncle Posey, you are wonderful surrogates who I love dearly, you always know when to call me. You represent a role model for married couples. Auntie Shirely thanks for your prayers, and Uncle Sonny for being a positive role model in my life. My sisters: Melonie, Roslyn, Rhoni, Robin and Brother Aulton, and to Hodari, Jendie, Mark, Marion, Richard and Alicia, Walter Allen, Chianty, Dewayne, Tanya, and Lauren may God continue to Bless our families. I love you all.

To: Rosager Parker, Pastors John & Gay Chisum, Pastor Julius Washington, Pastor Leon Jenkins, Bishops, B. A. Sanders; Newton & Myrna Hood, Donald Crumbley, Apostle Ron and Pastor Barbara Wilson and the entire FGCAI church family (Pastor Dave White, Pastor Terry Haynes, Pastor Tina Thomas, Pastor Ben Finey, Pastor Aaron Roberts, Elder Debra Vinson and Elder Sylvia Hampton); Metropolitan Community Church Family, Pastor Leon Perry, III, Pastor Emeritus Theodore Richardson, Rev. Ester Grier and the late Assistant Pastor Charles Gregory, Jim Matthews, Pastor Darryl Person, Janice Newell, Elaine Mann, Teresa Dismukes, Lacy Brown, Janice Price, Cheryl Van Eaton, Claudette Gregory, Calvin Giles, Gus Jones and the entire church family; thanks for your years of encouragement.

To: Apostle R. D. Henton, Bishop Charles Jones, Pastor Julius Willington M.B., Pastor John & Gay Chisum, Pastor ~Teacher William Lott, Bishop Charles Jones, Pastor Dr, Eleanor Miller, Rev. Patrice Beaman, Pastor Paul Jakes, Pastor Victor Walker, Rev. Richard Posey, Pastor Freddie Hill, Pastor Julius Rawls, Sr., the Nehemians, Pastor Marson and Vicky Johnson, Rev. Leon Coleman - Blessings to you for sowing a seed.

To the Catholic Archdiocese of Chicago: Auxilary Bishop Joseph. Perry, Pastor James Flynn, Pastor Lawrence Duris, and Pastor Richard Andrus, may the Lord continue to bless your Churches and Ministries. Thank you for trusting in me, we are charting new courses for the Glory of God.

Special thanks to Pastor David Bigsby of Calvery Baptist & Pastors Walter & Sandra Gillespie, Chosen Tabernacle Full Gospel Church. Praise God for all of you and if missed someone please count it to my head and not my heart. James and Shriley Wrightsell for your love and support. Thanks for your prayers and friendship.

GOD'S PLAN FOR AN ABUNDANT LIFE: Stewardship, Tithing & Discipleship

VASTT *Book Endorsements*

I have found the VASTT Ministry Stewardship Program to be the best program out there at this time for an appropriate parish tithing education that is biblically based while offering a formation in Christian discipleship resulting in proper stewardship on part of the Christian faithful....I appreciate the program for the fact that it is not a marketing strategy, nor an aggressive salesman pitch. Anton Seals is a genuine Christian devoted to service of the Lord and his Church. The VASTT exercise is meant to provide an education to a tithing ethic for your church members that will support your church and reap spiritual and material benefits for years to come.

Reverend Joseph N. Perry, Auxiliary Bishop
Chicago Roman Catholic Archdiocese of Chicago, Vicariate VI, South Holland, IL

...Brother Anton has a burden to see the church out of the curse of poverty and ignorance concerning the Word of God and His promises. He is a preacher and teacher with great insight and revelation in the word of God. The teaching from this book is practical and applicable. May God bless and use this book to bring increase in the kingdom of God.

Apostle Simpson Ngcizela. PhD   Senior Pastor and Overseer
Deeper Life Ministries Intnl., South Africa

...If you are looking for someone to encourage and inform your membership of the importance of building God's kingdom and how important stewardship is; Evangelist Seals is the man for you. His style of teaching and personal testimonies that he will share with the congregation will be an experience you will not forget. He has been a blessing to our church and we have adopted him as a son and we consider him as an honorary member of the Church of God in Christ.

Bishop B. A. Sanders,
The Church of God in Christ, Gary, IN

Evangelist Anton Seals, Sr...has many years of experience in Christian education. His commitment...was demonstrated... with Metropolitan Community Church. God's Plan for An Abundant Life ... is a work that will bless pastors and congregations by providing powerful vehicles for effective Stewardship."

Rev. Leon Perry, III. (Sr. Pastor)
Metropolitan Community Church, Chicago, IL

Evangelist Seals it is truly a marvelous work to see what God has done in your life as he prepared you for the writing of this wonderful manuscript that will bless God's people. We Praise God for your willingness to surrender to God to be a Hearer and a Doer of His Word. Your teaching on tithes and offerings has been a blessing to our Church family. We look forward to our continued Stewardship Journey as God has blessed us to move forward with the plans for our new Church home.

Pastor John Chisum and Co-Pastor Gay Chisum,
Gifts From God's Ministry, Chicago, IL

Minister Anton Seals has been blessed to receive divine inspiration from the Holy Spirit to comprise this book...a gift to the modern day church. The book is based on sound biblical teachings that challenge us to be obedient to the Word of God in the areas of Discipline, Stewardship and Tithing...takes a spiritual holistic approach that encompasses all aspects of our lives. This teaching has been a tremendous blessing to our ministry and has the potential to transform and revitalize the giving patterns in any ministry, regardless of denominational affiliation. This ministry message is life changing!

Pastor Julius K. Washington,
Greater Mount Tabor M. B. Church, Chicago, IL

VASTT *Book Endorsements (cont.)*

Passion is a driving force that can only be ignited by visionaries. Anton is a man of God who has a passion for the Body of Christ for stewardship standards to be promoted in our churches today. Anton is a living epistle who exemplifies how we should trust God for our increase. The Bible says, *"For whatsoever a man soweth, that shall he also reap."* (Gal. 6:7b) This manual will not only bless and inspire you, but will challenge you to bring into alliance everything that has to do with accountability... From our generation, God has raised up Minister Anton Seals who is not afraid to talk about money as it pertains to stewardship, because that is where our treasure lie.

Apostle Ron & Pastor Barbara Wilson
Full Gospel Christian Assemblies Int'l, Hazel Crest, IL

Thank you Minister Anton Seals and VASTT Ministry for the inspired teachings and training materials provided our church family during our Stewardship Campaign. Seeds of faith have been planted and now our tithes and offerings have increased…God's people are learning the benefits of giving His way. This is evidence by their reaping Heaven's blessings.

Pastor Leon Jenkins
Greater Salem Baptist Church, Chicago, IL

…We continue to be excited about what God has done through Minister Seals because the fire he lit continues to burn brightly…Today, we continue to rejoice at offering time! Minister Seals has made an indelible impression on the Mt. Sinai Church Family and we praise God that we will never be the same.

Rev. William R. Lott, Sr., Pastor/ Teacher,
Mt. Sinai M. B.Church, Chicago, IL

…Make no mistake about it this book accomplishes those tasks because it was written under God's Anointing…Yokes will be broken and hence lives will be changed after studying and meditating on the concepts and principals laid out in this review.

Assistant Pastor Richard Posey, III
Agape Family Life Center, Elgin, IL

What a blessing…It is our contention that your writings have the power to transform the Christian community in our giving and receiving, thus catapulting us to heights unknown …!

Pastor Marrion and Co-Pastor Vickie Johnson, Sr.
Come Alive Ministry of Faith, Chicago, IL.

"Umoja" means unity. We strive to maintain the unity of the spirit, the flow of brotherhood when love is shed abroad from heart to heart. That love, Agape - God kind of love, moves us to "Ujima", collective work and responsibility which is what Discipleship, Stewardship, Tithing and Offering are all about. VASTT Ministries, under the leadership of Evangelist Anton Seals, is shedding light on God's instructions for us to develop and prosper according to His Word, into a loving community ("Church"/"body") willingly taking care of God's Kingdom business.

Wasi Young, Executive Director
Umoja People, African Centered Programs

"Praise God from whom all blessings flow. It's truly an honor and privilege to utilize my creative gift to visually enhance this book. It is my prayer that everyone who reads this book will be richly blessed. What a wonderful blessing it has been working with Anton and Maxine Seals. May the Lord our God continue to bless and keep you both in all your endeavors as He continues to order your steps.

Michelle D. Muhammad
MDM Design, Graphic Design Services of Excellence & Integrity 708-868-1777

Introduction

God's Plan For An Abundant Life: Stewardship, Tithing & Discipleship

VASTT Ministry Is: A Ministry Consultant Service that provides Christian Educational Leadership services for churches and congregations in the area of Stewardship, Tithing and Discipleship. **The acronym "VASTT" means: Victory and Salvation Through Christ, the second T represents Jesus Christ Giving Up His Life On The Cross, for me.**

"God's Plan for an Abundant Life: Stewardship, Tithing and Discipleship" and the companion book, **"The ABC's For Organizing A Stewardship Journey"** are filled with spiritual principles based on sound biblical covenants and commandments written by the inspiration of the Holy Spirit. The second book is a training manual shared with Pastors and church leaders who allow VASTT Ministry to serve as their consultant for their Stewardship Journey. Churches going through the training have been blessed of God to harvest increases in their tithes and offering of 100, 60 and 30%. The doctrines are written for all denominations who believe in God the Father, the Son, the Resurrected Jesus, and the Holy Ghost, the triune God. **It is my prayer that the Lord will unlock the hidden treasures within you by convicting you to become, a vessel of faith, a tither, and not a robber or one who gives cheap tips.**

This manual edifies, exhorts, and comforts the Body of Christ, to trust in the Godly Principles for Living An Abundant Life. By implementing the principals outlined in these two manuals, the life of the congregation will be transformed. The Pastor, church leaders, and the congregation will realize a paradigm shift within their church family when they collectively undertake this Stewardship Journey. Testimonies of miracles and wondrous praises will abound throughout.

One of the greatest challenges facing the church today is the lack of monies; (tithes and offerings) collected every Sunday. Too many pastors are reluctant to or have failed to teach tithes and offerings to their congregations. Therefore, people are unwilling to sow a seed of one tenth, which is the tithe. Too many church believers fail to bring their tithes and offerings to the storehouse that there may be meat in my (God's) house.

> **Malachi 3:-10-12** *Bring ye all the tithes into the storehouse, that there may be meat in mine house, and prove me now herewith, saith the Lord of hosts, if I will not open you the windows of heaven, and pour you out a blessing, that there shall not be room enough to receive it. 11 And I will rebuke the devourer for your sakes, and he shall not destroy the fruits of your ground; neither shall your vine cast her fruit before the time in the field, saith the Lord of hosts. 12 And all nations shall call you blessed: for ye shall be a delightsome land, saith the Lord of hosts.*

People are worshipping money more than they value God. Failure to teach congregations the will of God concerning tithes and offerings has left us spiritually bankrupt and on barren land. Equal sacrifice, not equal giving, pleases the Lord. Special fund-raisers outside of tithing create spirits of dependency to trust carnal wisdom verses Godly wisdom. There is a difference between raising funds for the Lord and fundraiser. The children of God must have faith that God will rebuke the devourer, and provide their every need.

Introduction
God's Plan For An Abundant Life: Stewardship, Tithing & Discipleship

God's Plan For An Abundant Life addresses three basic principles. Prayerfully, this work-book will help you:

1. To become disciplined by God's Word, as hearers and doers of God's Word

2. To remain faithful and excited about giving back to God your tithes and offerings

3. To know that God created us as stewards with power to care for all He created

When studied and lived by, these principles will change the course of your Life. VASTT Ministry challenges you to trust God to smite your debt, for the Word of God says:

Beloved, I wish above all things that thou mayest prosper and be in health, even as thy soul prospereth. There is not a better plan, than God's Plan to help people reduce their personal and congregational debt, **John 1:2.**

There is a Goliath in the land today, and his name is Credit Card and he has a band of warriors called Debt and Stress. Their first cousins are Frustration and Depression. The prince of this world causes debt, stress, frustration, and depression. Jesus said we have Victory over satan and the wiles of the devil. People have tried every gimmick and every plan known to man to raise money for the church and to get out of our personal debt. So why are we still in bondage and slaves to our debt? These worldly spirits come to fulfill the lust of flesh. Debt devours the foundation of our families, communities and our physical well-being. We are driven to work long hours and for longer years. We are paying more but actually having less. We give God nothing or we bring token gifts to the altar to tip God.

God is a jealous God; he wants you to serve him with all your heart, mind, soul and strength, placing no other God before him. We cannot serve mammon and God. We will love the first and hate the latter. Do you value your debt more than you value God? Look at your personal checkbook. List where you spend the money you are blessed to have. How much do you pay in interest? How long have you been paying on a small credit card debt, and at what interest rate? Our checkbooks and receipts tell us where our values lie. Is it more than what you give to God? Tithing demonstrates our willingness to give God what he commanded us to give, our tithes and offerings. The level of your giving determines the value of who/what you worship. The church is the storehouse, the temple of God, where we are to bring our tithes and offerings. What does your tithing account tell God about you?

Tithing brings order into the Body of Christ. You cannot beat God giving, for the Lord loves a cheerful giver. You really are a chosen people of a royal priesthood. You shall be blessed coming in and blessed going out, and the seed of the seed and the fruit of the seed shall inherit the promise that God gave to Abraham. You are the seed of Abraham. Giving your tithes and offering is a response of obedience to the command of God. **Your abundant blessings are directly related to your personal relationship with the Lord through your prayers, faith, and obedient life according to the Word of God.**

Remember that the believers and non-believers, the saved and the un-saved, the churched and the un-churched, and the lost and the found; are all God's children. Never forget where the Lord brought you from, so take the mote out of your eyes so that you can really see through the eyes of our Lord, what he has promised to the faithful and obedient children of God.

May this book bless you as it has blessed me and my family. Open the Wells.

GOD'S PLAN FOR AN ABUNDANT LIFE: Stewardship, Tithing & Discipleship

Seminar 1

Stewards
Are God's Anointed Managers

Evangelist Anton L. Seals, Sr.
VASTT Ministry

Copyright © 2002 VASTT Ministry & Publishing

GOD'S PLAN FOR AN ABUNDANT LIFE: Stewardship, Tithing & Discipleship

Outline of Seminar 1

Stewardship Characteristics: Stewards Are God's Anointed Managers

Stewards Have A Fruitful Inheritance	20-27
Stewards Are Not Jealous and Selfish	28-09
Stewards Are Accountable:	30-31
Stewards Serve God and Manage Wealth Wisely	32
Stewards Have Power To Get Wealth	32-33
Stewards Lay There Treasures In Heaven	33
Stewards Seek The Righteousness of God	33
Stewards Willingly Give	34
Stewards Are Faithful and Know How To Pray	34-35
Stewards Are Not Hypocrites	35
Stewards Are Faithful of The Talents	36-37
Stewards Are Entrusted With God's Mysteries	38
Stewards Know When and How To Collect	39-40
Stewards Are Not Greedy	40
Stewards Have Strength and Are Content	40
Steward Are Filled With Grace	41
Stewards Provide for The Church	42
Stewards Know How To Sow and Give Willingly	42-43
Stewards Are Not Deceitful	44
Stewards Are Transformed	44

GOD'S PLAN FOR AN ABUNDANT LIFE: Stewardship, Tithing & Discipleship

A Plan For An Abundant Life

The training that you are embarking upon has been developed for the sole purpose of assisting your Pastor(s) to water the seeds that have been planted for both your spiritual growth and the Corporate Body of Christ. It is our goal to richly enhance the level of commitment of church leaders, who are willing vessels, and who Love the Lord with all of their Hearts, Minds and Souls, Deut. 6: 2-5. We pray that the Light of God, Mt. 5:14, be seen in your obedience to live according to the Word of God. If you truly love the Lord there will be a tremendous transformation, Rm. 8:29, of how you willingly give to God your:

- **TIME:** To Pray & Fast; for Praise & Worship and to Serve God
- **TALENTS:** Discovering and using your Spiritual Gifts for His Glory
- **TREASURES:** Giving of your money through tithes and offerings.

We can never beat God's Giving, Luke 6:38. God does not need your money. The Cattle on a thousand Hills is mine said the Lord, Psalm 50:10. However, He commands you to bring your tithes and offerings with a willing heart (Ex. 35:5) to His Storehouse (Malachi 3:10), for the Lord loves a cheerful giver (2 Corth. 9:7). It is God's desire to destroy the devourer so that he can bless us. You must never stop giving your best for the Lord, for it is better to give than to receive (Acts 20:35). When you become a tither with a willing heart you serve at a higher level of excellence, for God brings order into your life. There will be a shift in your relationship with Christ Jesus, and you are transformed (Romans 12:2) into a new creature in Christ. The old man has died and passed away (2 Corth. 5:17; Col. 3:10, 12). **You have received the anointing that destroys the devourer, and you no longer have a mind that finds lame excuses to justify why and how you rob God.** Discover your Treasures in your Earthen Vessel, 2 Corth 4:7, and allow God the Father, through His Son Jesus Christ, to release the Abundant Blessings, which are laid up for the true believers who keep His Word, commandments, Deut. 28-1-14. He holds in His hands the keys that will open your treasure chest stored in His Storehouse, called Blessed Assurance. If Sons of God then you are Heirs to the Kingdom of God, Rms. 8:17 and where God is there is peace, joy, happiness, love, and His Riches in Glory. Remember, He is the Owner and you are the Disciples that have been given Divine Stewardship to Manage: with Wisdom, what He has blessed you with. It all belongs to God, you have been given His sacred *Trust* to manage.

> **God is the Owner and you are the Disciples that have been given Divine Stewardship to Manage, with Wisdom.**

Copyright © 2002 VASTT Ministry & Publishing

13

GOD'S PLAN FOR AN ABUNDANT LIFE: Stewardship, Tithing & Discipleship

Purpose of Manual

This Stewardship Workbook is part one of a four part series used for Leadership Training on Stewardship - Tithing - Discipleship & How To Organize A Stewardship Journey. The primary focus of this training manual is to provide a holistic approach for training church leadership and congregations according to what God says about your tithes and offerings, and the giving of your **Time, Talents, and Treasures**. The training includes instructions on the invaluable elements of:

1. **Stewardship**
    a. The Divine Creation of Man: As Stewards(ship)
    b. Stewards Over What God Has Given To You
    c. Stewards of God's Earthly Kingdom
    d. Seek Ye First The Kingdom Of God and His Righteous

2. **Tithing:**
    a. Ownership of God
    b. Giving your Tithes and Offerings
    c. Sowing and Harvesting

3. **Discipleship**
    a. Living According To God's Word
    b. Becoming a Living Epistle
    c. A Servant's Heart (Bondservant)

MISSION:

Teaching God's Word and Commandments as the foundational principles for stewardship, tithing, discipleship, and the abundant life provided for believers who fear God, obey His Word, and are doers of His Word, James 1:22. You must establish these principles as a foundation of the churches spiritual and fiscal plan for: building and maintaining the House of God; spreading the Gospel of Jesus Christ, Mt. 28-18-20; and for meeting the needs of the poor and afflicted, Is. 61-3; Luke 4:18.

> **Deut. 8:18:** *But thou shalt remember the Lord thy God: for it is he that giveth thee power to get wealth, that he may establish his covenant which he sware unto thy fathers, as it is this day (KJV).*
>
> **Malachi 3:10** *Bring ye all the tithes into the storehouse, that there may be meat in mine house, and prove me now herewith, saith the Lord of hosts, if I will not open you the windows of heaven, and pour you out a blessing, that there shall not be room enough to receive it.*
>
> **Luke 6:38** *Give, and it shall be given unto you; good measure, pressed down, and shaken together, and running over, shall men give into your bosom. For with the same measure that ye mete withal it shall be measured to you again.*

GOD'S PLAN FOR AN ABUNDANT LIFE: Stewardship, Tithing & Discipleship

Defining Stewardship

The writings reflected, revealed, and shared in this manual are provided by the inspiration of the Holy Spirit. The word **stewardship** comes from the root word **Steward.** *The word means to be over, in charge as to manage, to give direction, to serve as the* overseer, and to supervise and care for the very things of God. **We therefore must come to recognize the higher calling of God on our lives.** We were not only called to praise and glorify God but to be held accountable and responsible for the heavenly treasures God has given to us, upon this, his earthly paradise, for heaven on earth experiences.

The creation of Adam and Eve demonstrates again the awesome power of God. It was God's will and plan to create Man in His Image (Let Us Make). He has given us **Dominion**, all power, **dunamis power**.

> In Greek **dunamis** means: force, spec. miraculous power, a miracle itself: ability, abundance, meaning, might, (worker of) miracle(-s), power, strength, violence, mighty (wonderful) work.

When we study the creation we must also recognize the orderly process of which he created the universe and man. The creation of man (Adam) from the earth, means Adamah in Hebrew. There is a direct relationship to our existence and that of the soil of the earth that we live on and manage for God. *This basic concept of giving began with God creating the world and giving man dominion over the world.* Man's creation was the final triumph of God's Creation, and the birth and crucifixion of Jesus is also part of Alpha and Omega.

Man was given power and held accountable and responsible for the stewardship of all God's creations. God clearly states in:

> **Genesis 1:26** And God said, Let us make man in our image, after our likeness: and let them have dominion over the fish of the sea, and over the fowl of the air, and over the cattle, and over all the earth, and over every creeping thing that creepeth upon the earth.

Stewards of God are therefore created in the image of God, the Son, and the Holy Ghost. We are given power that illustrated God's covenant with Abraham, in Gen 17. Therefore as stewards of God we must exemplify the very character of God. Stewardship qualities are fundamental of characteristics of God's Disciples, who have accepted Jesus Christ as their Lord and Savior and live a disciplined life for Christ, according to his Word.

GOD'S PLAN FOR AN ABUNDANT LIFE: Stewardship, Tithing & Discipleship

Defining Stewardship

When God created Adam he gave him dominion over the entire land. He was the sole proprietor of the earth. God had given him supernatural intelligence doused and rooted in God's revelation. God gave him wisdom, knowledge, and understanding. As we refer to Adam, man, this in no way excludes Women (Eve), for it is non-gender specific. In Genesis 1:26, "God said Let us make man in our image, after our likeness; and then let him have dominion ….upon the earth." Genesis 1:27 repeats God's intent by declaring "So God created man in his own image, in the image of God created he him; male and female created he them. We were created to multiply, and to be rulers, care-takers, care-givers, (providers), builders, creators, developers, and defenders of God's universe. We were created by God to serve as his chief Stewards and servants. We are created in His honor and with favor.

> **Without the spirit in us we would not exist. It is the soul of man that we find the Spirit of God embodied in.**

God's honor for the creation of man, the Word made flesh, is illustrated by his declaration "Let Us Make Man", referencing three persons of the divine counsel known as the Trinity (Triune God): Father, Son, and Holy Ghost. Clearly man was created to honor and devote his life to God for all that has given to him. Man was created to manage the world as Stewards.

Job 38:4 *Where wast thou when I laid the foundations of the earth? declare, if thou hast understanding.*

God has given you power to manage this world system. You have been given revelation power, divine wisdom, knowledge and understanding. God also gave man favor by making him higher than the other creatures. God gave you both a spiritual and natural creation to demonstrate His favor on mankind. Without the spirit in us we would not exist. For it is in the soul of man that we find the Spirit of God embodied in.

2 Cor. 4:7 *But we have this treasure in earthen vessels, that the excellency of the power may be of God, and not of us.*

The soul of man is the Spirit of God in His image that is immortal, but it has the embodiment of intelligence, will, and emotions. Concealed within me, all of us, is a treasure in an earthen vessel, that is not of us, but of the excellence of the power of God in us. **If man would live a life filled with faith and obedience, that leads to trust in the truth of His Word, then we could open the treasures of God's revelation power, receive the abundant blessings, and all the promises found in his covenant with Abraham and the seed of his seed.**

GOD'S PLAN FOR AN ABUNDANT LIFE: Stewardship, Tithing & Discipleship

Defining Stewardship

It is God's unwarranted favor (grace) and mercy that allows mankind the free will to live life as he chooses. Our flesh is carnal-minded and is enmity to God. It is impossible for man to understand or to know how to please God, for the flesh minds the things of the flesh. Paul teaches that man can not live by flesh alone.

> **Romans 8:4-6** *That the righteousness of the law might be fulfilled in us, who walk not after the flesh, but after the Spirit. [5] For they that are after the flesh do mind the things of the flesh; but they that are after the Spirit the things of the Spirit. [6] For to be carnally minded is death; but to be spiritually minded is life and peace. [7] Because the carnal mind is enmity against God: for it is not subject to the law of God, neither indeed can be.*
>
> **2 Corth. 5:7** *(For we walk by faith, not by sight:)*

Unfortunately, our now time present day society does not acknowledge nor fear the awesome power of God, the Creator, who has given us life and power over our daily lives.

This workbook on Stewardship will help you discover who you really are and why you were created to be a Steward. Explore Genesis 1:28 and see the **four major defining principles that establish the purpose and responsibility of man:**

> **Genesis 1:28** *And God blessed them, and God said unto them, Be fruitful, and multiply, and replenish the earth, and subdue it: and have dominion over the fish of the sea, and over the fowl of the air, and over every living thing that moveth upon the earth.*

1. To Be Fruitful

2. To Multiply

3. To Replenish the earth

4. To Subdue the earth (Land)

GOD'S PLAN FOR AN ABUNDANT LIFE: Stewardship, Tithing & Discipleship

Defining Stewardship

Man was given ***dominion** and every need was provided. In verse Gen.1:29 and 30: "And God said, Behold, I have given you every herb bearing seed, which is upon the face of all the earth, and every tree, in the which is the fruit of a tree yielding seed; **to you it shall be for meat**. And to every beast of the earth, and to every fowl of the air, and to every thing that creepeth upon the earth, wherein there is life, I have given every green herb for meat: and it was so.

In Genesis 1:30, to you it shall be for meat. God set and established man to rule over his earthly kingdom providing a flourishing agricultural system and the onset of a world economic system that man was to manage.

To help you understand the powerful implications identified within this subject, brief definitions and explanations of some key words are provided.

The word **principle** according to Webster is translated: *the ultimate source, origin, or cause of something. It is also a natural or original tendency, faculty, or endowment.*

Principles, therefore, are fundamental truths, laws, doctrines, or motivating forces, (we are talking about the forces of God and His Power), upon which others are based as in moral character.

> ***Dominion** in Hebrew is translated **radah, raw-daw'**: to tread down, subjugate; specifically to crumble off: come to, make to have rule over or control of, to prevail against, reign, (bear, make to rule). (Strong's)
>
> ***Dominion** in Greek is translated **dunamis**: power, all power.

Meat in Hebrew is translated oklah, ok-law'; food :- consume, devour, eat, food, meat. This meat, the seed, provides provisions for man. In Greek **steward** is defined as (**oikonomos; oykonomos**) which means a house distributor, manager, overseer, by extension, the fiscal agent –treasurer; an employee in that capacity; figurative a preacher (of the Gospel):- chamberlain, and or governor, a steward.

GOD'S PLAN FOR AN ABUNDANT LIFE: Stewardship, Tithing & Discipleship

Defining Stewardship

Steward, also defined in the Webster dictionary means:

1. a person put in charge of the affairs of a large household or estate, whose duties include supervision of the kitchen and the servants, management of household accounts, etc.

2. one who acts as a supervisor or administrator, as of finances and property, for another or others.

3. A person variously responsible for the food, drink, service personnel, etc., in a club, restaurant, etc.

4. an attendant, as on a ship, train, etc., employed to look after the passengers' comfort; flight attendant

5. an officer on a ship who is in charge of stores and culinary arrangements

6. a person morally responsible for the careful use of money, time, talents, or other resources, esp. with respect to the principles or needs of a community or group, [our responsibility as stewards of the earth's resources, to act as a steward, a steward of (something);

> **Christians have a spiritual debtor-ship to the whole world, a holy trusteeship in the gospel, and a binding stewardship in their possessions**

God is the source of all blessings, temporal and spiritual; all that we have and are we owe to Him. Christians have a spiritual debtor-ship to the whole world, a holy trusteeship in the gospel, and a binding stewardship in their possessions. You are therefore under obligation to serve Him with your Time, Talents, and material possessions, (Treasures). You should recognize all these as entrusted to you for the Glory of God and for helping others as they seek to know Jesus. According to the Scriptures, Christians should contribute of their means cheerfully, regularly, systematically, proportionately, and liberally for the advancement of the Redeemer's cause on earth.

It should be obvious what God is saying to us about giving, managing, accountability, and responsibility for the abundant blessings we receive.

GOD'S PLAN FOR AN ABUNDANT LIFE: Stewardship, Tithing & Discipleship

What Kind Of Steward Are You?

What kind of Steward are you?

All believers/stewards are responsible for supporting the church by becoming better stewards, managers, and overseers, of the vast blessings provided by God. We are to take the Gospel and spread it across the world, Matthew 28:18-20. When we fail to give God our tithes and offerings we are not obeying the Word of God. When we fail to give our tithes we are living in disobedience and not performing the duties and responsibilities as outlined by God in the Bible. Your failure to support the church is not only blocking and delaying your blessings, but it is also hindering the spreading of the Gospel of Jesus Christ to the entire world. Paul clearly defines what the Word of God had to say about stewardship and the collection to support the church. In I Corinthians 16:1-2, Paul teaches the church how and when to give.

In Genesis 4:1-6, we read the story of the two sons of Adam and Eve who are stewards. Here we will find a revealing story about the types of giving in the story of Cain and Able, illustrating how to give an offering to God. This does not demonstrate the first instance of tithing. It does, however, clearly establish one of the first examples of man giving an offering to God. There is a difference between the offerings given by the two brothers, Cain and Able. The attitude of the varying conditions of the human heart and mind are demonstrated in Genesis 4:1-6.

Stewardship Characteristics:

1. Stewards Have A Fruitful Inheritance: Genesis 1:28-30; 2 Peter 1:1-11

2. Stewards Are Not Jealous and Selfish   Genesis 4:3-5, John 13:34

3. Stewards Are Accountable: I Corth. 4:1; Luke 16:1-13; Romans:14:11,12; Hebrews 13:16-17; Rev. 20:11-12.

4. Stewards Serve God and Manage Wealth Wisely: Luke 16:9-13 (GW); Luke 16:9-13 (KJ)

5. Stewards Have Power To Get Wealth: Deut. 8:18; 28:1-14; Ecc. 10:19, Proverb 10:22

GOD'S PLAN FOR AN ABUNDANT LIFE: Stewardship, Tithing & Discipleship

What Kind Of Steward Are You?

6. Stewards Lay Their Treasures In Heaven: Matthew 6:19-20

7. Stewards Seek The Righteousness of God: Matthew 6:33-34

8. Stewards Willingly Give: Matthew 6:1-4; Acts 20:33-35

9. Stewards Are Faithful Know How To Pray: Matthew 6:5-13

10. Stewards Are Not Hypocrites: Matthew 23: 23-28

11. Faithful Stewards of The Talents: Matthew 25:14-30 Matthew 25:31-46

12. Stewards Entrusted God's With God's Mysteries: 1 Cor. 4:1-2

13. Stewards Know When and How To Collect: 1 Corinthians 16:1-3; 2 Chron. 24:6; 2 Chron. 24:9

14. Stewards Are Not Greedy: Luke 12:16-21

15. Stewards Have Strength and Are Content: Philip. 4:10-13

16. Stewards of Grace: 1 Peter 4:10

17. Stewards Provide for The Church: 1 Cor. 9:1-9; 1 Tim. 5:18

18. Stewards Know How To Sow (Give) Sow and Give Equally With Grace: 2 Cor. 8:1-12; 2 Cor. 8:13-16; 2 Cor. 9:1-15

19. Stewards Are Not Deceitful: Acts 5:1-11

20. Stewards Are Transformed: Romans 12:1-2

Copyright © 2002 VASTT Ministry & Publishing

GOD'S PLAN FOR AN ABUNDANT LIFE: Stewardship, Tithing & Discipleship

God's Plan For Stewardship

God's Plan for Stewardship:

To help you understand the inherent gifts, power, and authority born within you, the following exercise is designed to help the reader understand: Who You Are, Whose You Are and Why You Were Created.

The creation of man was the last act of God in creating the World as we know it today. Man was made in the image of God and given dominion.

A. On Pages 11-15 of this workbook you will find the definitions for steward(s):

    1. What is a Steward? _____
_____

    2. What is a Steward responsible for?_____
_____

    3. Are you held accountable and responsible for the manifold blessings given to you by God? _____. Explain _____
_____

    4. What kind of Steward are You? _____
_____

B. Read Genesis 1:26-30:

And God said, Let us make man in our image, after our likeness: and let them have dominion over the fish of the sea, and over the fowl of the air, and over the cattle, and over all the earth, and over every creeping thing that creepeth upon the earth. [27] So God created man in his own image, in the image of God created he him; male and female created he them. [28] And God blessed them, and God said unto them, Be fruitful, and multiply, and replenish the earth, and subdue it: and have dominion over the fish of the sea, and over the fowl of the air, and over every living thing that moveth upon the earth. [29] And God said, Behold, I have given you every herb bearing seed, which is upon the face of all the earth, and every tree, in the which is the fruit of a tree yielding seed; to you it shall be for meat. [30] And to every beast of the earth, and to every fowl of the air, and to every thing that creepeth upon the earth, wherein there is life, I have given every green herb for meat: and it was so.

God's Plan For Stewardship

C. Answer the following questions: (Answers are found in Gen. 1:26-30)

1. Who created man? _____ in his own image.

2. Let us make _____ in our _____ after our _____.

3. Let them have _____.

4. In verse 28 God blessed then and said unto them to be _____, and _____, and _____ the earth and _____ it.

5. What did God give to man for food? _____

6. What did God give us over the earth? _____

7. Paul teaches in Romans 8:17 that if we are heirs of the seed of Abraham, then if children, then heirs; heirs of God, and joint-heirs with Christ; if so be that we suffer with him, that we may be also glorified together.

8. Whose are You? (See Romans 8:17)
    a. Are you an heir of the seed of Abraham? Yes ___ or No ___
    b. Then if children, then _____, heirs of _____ and joint-heirs with _____. If you suffer with him you may also be _____ together.

9. 1 John 3:1 See how great a love the Father has bestowed upon us, that we should be _____ _____ of _____ and such we are. For this _____ the world _____ know us, because it _____ _____ know _____.

GOD'S PLAN FOR AN ABUNDANT LIFE: Stewardship, Tithing & Discipleship

Study Sheets:
Stewardship Characteristics

I. Stewards Are Given A Fruitful Inheritance:

A. According to the Webster's New World Dictionary fruitful means:
- **To bear much, increase, and grow,**
- **To produce much, to be productive, to be prolific**
- **To be fertile, and profitable**

As you have read repeatedly in this manual God's intention from your initial creation was to give you the ability to be productive by providing you with the World's Agricultural System. You may ask, Why did God wait to create man last on the sixth day? God wanted to show you (man) that waiting on Him allows you to be prepared for all the wonderful blessings that are laid up for mankind. As stewards you are to be productive by bringing an increase in all that you do. It is the Blessing of God unto you of Salvation, giving you an anointing for prosperity and success. 3 John 1:2, Beloved, I wish above all things that thou mayest prosper and be in health, even as thy soul prospereth.

B. Paul teaches in Ephesians 1:3 that God blessed us with all Spiritual Blessings:

> **In this exercise read the following information on Spiritual Blessings, and fill in the blanks. To complete this section you must read Ephesians 1:1-7**

> **1. Spiritual Blessings** result in your being fruitful and abundantly blessed. You cannot be fruitful in life if you are not connected to the creator of your Spiritual and physical DNA. In John 15 we learn the importance of Abiding in the Vine, for we are the branch.

> Throughout the world sin is running rampant. Man has failed to acknowledge and Fear the Power of God. We live in a world where the evidence of the sins from Adam and Eve's era, are part of the continuing curse that God placed on man. Yet, by the Redeeming Blood of Jesus, the righteous can inherit bountiful blessings, based on their personal, intimate relationship with Christ, by living according to His Word. You must first Seek the Righteousness of God, Mt 6:33.

GOD'S PLAN FOR AN ABUNDANT LIFE: Stewardship, Tithing & Discipleship

Study Sheets:
Stewardship Characteristics

C. This exercise is to help you understand the importance of who you are and how blessed you really are. Complete this exercise by filling in the correct words from the scriptures listed below: have a group discussion regarding what these scriptures mean to you.

1. Ephesians 1:3-7; 11-14

_____ be the God and Father of our Lord Jesus Christ, who hath blessed us with all _____ _____ in _____ places in _____. [4] According as He hath _____ us in him _____ the _____ of the _____, that we should be _____ and _____ blame before him in _____: [5] Having _____ us unto the _____ of children by Jesus Christ to _____, according to the good pleasure of his _____, [6] To the praise of the _____ of his _____, wherein he hath made us _____ in the _____ [7] In whom we have _____ through his _____, the _____ of sins, according to the _____ of his grace. [11] In whom also we have _____ an _____, being _____ according to the purpose of him who worketh all things after the counsel of his own will: [12] That we should be to the _____ of his glory, who first _____ in Christ. [13] In whom ye also trusted, after that ye heard the word of truth, the gospel of your_____: in whom also after that ye believed, ye were _____ with that Holy Spirit of promise, [14] Which is the earnest of our inheritance until the redemption of the _____ _____, unto the praise of his glory.

GOD'S PLAN FOR AN ABUNDANT LIFE: Stewardship, Tithing & Discipleship

Study Sheets:
Stewardship Characteristics

D. In Ephesians 1: 3-7, 11-14 there are nine things that God has done for us:

1. Blessed us (v 3)	6. Abound toward us (v 8)
2. Chosen us (v 3)	7. Made known unto us (v 9)
3. Predestinated us (v 5, 11)	8. Given us an inheritance (v 11, 14)
4. Made us accepted (v 6)	9. Sealed us (v 13)
5. Redeemed us (v 7)	

Additional research shows that God blessed us with His True Riches that you can study latter: (Dakes Bible Reference)

- Riches of His grace (Eph 1:7)

- Riches of the glory of the inheritance in the saints (believers) (Eph. 1:18)

- Un-searchable riches of Christ (Eph. 3:8)

- Riches of His glory (Eph. 3:16; Romans 9:23)

- Riches of His goodness (Rom 2:4)

- Riches of wisdom and knowledge (Rom. 11:33)

- Riches in glory (Phil. 4:19)

- Riches of the Glory of the mystery of Christ in you (Col. 1:27)

- Riches of the full assurance of understanding God's mystery (Col.2:2)

- Reproach of Christ greater riches than in Egypt (Heb. 11:26)

Study Sheets: Stewardship Characteristics

E. John teaches in John 15: 5-10 key points that stewards must acknowledge as they continue to grow in their daily walk with Christ.

Read the following scriptures found in John 15 before trying to fill in the blanks for the next questions:

John 15:5,7 -10 — *[5]. I am the vine, ye are the branches: He that abideth in me, and I in him, the same bringeth forth much fruit: for without me ye can do nothing. [7] If ye abide in me, and my words abide in you, ye shall ask what ye will, and it shall be done unto you. [8] Herein is my Father glorified, that ye bear much fruit; so shall ye be my disciples. [9] As the Father hath loved me, so have I loved you: continue ye in my love. [10] If ye keep my commandments, ye shall abide in my love; even as I have kept my Father's commandments, and abide in his love.*

a. Who is the vine?_____, **b.** Who are the Branches? _____

c. Who Abideth in you? _____ **d.** Who shall bring forth much fruit? _____, **e.** Without **f.** _____ you can do **g.** _____. **h.** If _____ abide in _____, **i.** And _____ _____ abide in _____, **j.** Who shall ask what they will? _____, **k.** and it _____ be _____ unto you. **l.** Who gets the Glory? _____ and who shall be the disciples? _____ **m.** Explain what is meant by as the father has loved me, so I have loved you? _____ **n.** If you keep his _____, what will happen?

o. How do I keep his love? _____.

GOD'S PLAN FOR AN ABUNDANT LIFE: Stewardship, Tithing & Discipleship

Study Sheets:
Stewardship Characteristics

F. Stewards Know Who Provides The Increase:

1 Cor. 3:5-13: *Who then is Paul, and who is Apollos, but ministers by whom ye believed, even as the Lord gave to every man? [6] I have planted, Apollos watered; but God gave the increase. [7] So then neither is he that planteth any thing, neither he that watereth; but God that giveth the increase. [8] Now he that planteth and he that watereth are one: and every man shall receive his own reward according to his own labour. [9] For we are labourers together with God: ye are God's husbandry, ye are God's building. [10] According to the grace of God which is given unto me, as a wise masterbuilder, I have laid the foundation, and another buildeth thereon. But let every man take heed how he buildeth thereupon. [11] For other foundation can no man lay than that is laid, which is Jesus Christ. [12] Now if any man build upon this foundation gold, silver, precious stones, wood, hay, stubble; [13] Every man's work shall be made manifest: for the day shall declare it, because it shall be revealed by fire; and the fire shall try every man's work of what sort it is.*

> *Now he that planteth and he that watereth are one: and every man shall receive his own reward according to his own labour. For we are labourers together with God…*

2 Peter 1:1-11 *Simon Peter, a servant and an apostle of Jesus Christ, to them that have obtained like precious faith with us through the righteousness of God and our Saviour Jesus Christ: [2] Grace and peace be multiplied unto you through the knowledge of God, and of Jesus our Lord, [3] According as his divine power hath given unto us all things that pertain unto life and godliness, through the knowledge of him that hath called us to glory and virtue: [4] Whereby are given unto us exceeding great and precious promises: that by these ye might be partakers of the divine nature, having escaped the corruption that is in the world through lust.[5] And beside this, giving all diligence, add to your faith virtue; and to virtue knowledge; [6] And to knowledge temperance; and to temperance patience; and to patience godliness; [7] And to godliness brotherly kindness; and to brotherly kindness charity. [8] For if these things be in you, and abound, they make you that ye shall neither be barren nor unfruitful in the knowledge of our Lord Jesus Christ. [9] But he that lacketh these things is blind, and cannot see afar off, and hath forgotten that he was purged from his old sins. [10] Wherefore the rather, brethren, give diligence to make your calling and election sure: for if ye do these things, ye shall never fall: [11] For so an entrance shall be ministered unto you abundantly into the everlasting kingdom of our Lord and Saviour Jesus Christ.*

GOD'S PLAN FOR AN ABUNDANT LIFE: Stewardship, Tithing & Discipleship

Study Sheets:
Stewardship Characteristics

G. Spiritual Inheritance- Chosen and Predestined Blessings From God:
When God gave his blessing to man he gave you His inheritance for His Glory. Look up the words: Give, Gave, and Giving to help you understand the importance of giving in your life.

1. To stimulate your thinking answer the following questions: What is God giving you?
_____
_____

What has God given you?
_____
_____

God gave you What?
_____
_____

What have you given God?
_____
_____

What are you giving to God?
_____
_____

What Have You Given Back To God?
_____
_____

> **Giving** is defined according to Webster's Dictionary as: To make a present of, to deliver, or recompense, as in being redeemed- bought with a price, to provide, inflict, administer, manifest (to show), award, designate, devote, apply, specify, sacrifice, devote, perform, submit, and to cause to take place.....

Study Sheets:
Stewardship Characteristics

2. To receive what God already has prepared and promised for you, there are some requirements. Open your bibles to the following scriptures:

In Luke 6:38 we know that this is actually the Word of God for it is written in Red. Luke 6:38 *Give, and it shall be given unto you; good measure, pressed down, and shaken together, and running over, shall men give into your bosom. For with the same measure that ye mete withal it shall be measured to you again.*

1. What does the Word say will happen when you give? _____
_____
_____
_____

2. How shall men give unto your bosom?
_____
_____
_____

4. What does your giving have to do with what you get back?

Explaining the blessings of God are awesome, yet we often overlook the greatest gifts given to us. To this end many of you do not know what your spiritual gift(s) is (are). We even take them for granted, not knowing that they are given to us for the glory of God and for edifying the Body of Christ. Because you are created in the likeness and image of God, who is both a Loving and Giving God, one of your gifts is giving with a cheerful heart. Cheerful and giving are powerful descriptive words that require action and commitment. When you read the book of Genesis you will notice that God, the Creator, Blessed us by giving us **dominion**, His image and likeness. Please notice that the entire Bible is predicated on God giving to man for his Glory. When you think again of the awesomeness of God, do a self- introspection to see if your life reflects a heart

Study Sheets: Stewardship Characteristics

and spirit of giving. Does your life line up with the will of God? You can not beat God Giving, so why are you Robbing God? Here are some examples of God giving grace to you: He created you, gave you his likeness and image, with all power to be: fruitful, multiply, replenish and subdue the land, made us sons and children of God, giving us his wisdom, knowledge and understanding, that we may lead others to Christ. God gave you his only begotten Son Jesus, who shed His blood and gave up his life, dying on Calvary, that you might have eternal life; giving you the fruit of the spirit and equipping you with spiritual weapons to stand against the wiles of the prince of this world. God gave you the ability to love, while having grace and mercy by the anointing and the in-filling of the Holy Spirit to be both the salt and the light of His World. Your life must be given to lead others to the path of righteousness, helping others to find their way out of darkness and into the wonderful light, and yes leading then to want to know Jesus. By the blood of Jesus your sins are forgiven, when you confess with your mouth that He is the Son of the Living God, he will make you a New Creature in Christ Jesus.

Your life must be given to lead others to the path of righteousness, helping others to find their way out of darkness and into the wonderful light, and yes leading then to want to know Jesus.

Explain:_____

_____
_____
_____
_____
_____
_____
_____

GOD'S PLAN FOR AN ABUNDANT LIFE: Stewardship, Tithing & Discipleship

Study Sheets:
Stewardship Characteristics

II. Stewards Are Not Jealous and Selfish:

As you think about giving back to God, are your thoughts driven by vanity, selfishness and to be seen as prosperous in the flesh, but yet bankrupt in spiritual growth? Are you a person who is easily discouraged and jealous because someone has more than you, or appears to be more blessed than you? Read the following Scriptures to see how these types of attitudes and thought processes are so dangerous and are blocking your spiritual blessing. Keep in mind the Love of God:

> **John 13:34-35** *A new commandment I give unto you, That ye love one another; as I have loved you, that ye also love one another. [35] By this shall all men know that ye are my disciples, if ye have love one to another.*

> **Genesis 4:3-5** *And in process of time it came to pass, that Cain brought of the fruit of the ground an offering unto the Lord. [4] And Abel, he also brought of the firstlings of his flock and of the fat thereof. And the Lord had respect unto Abel and to his offering: [5] But unto Cain and to his offering he had not respect. And Cain was very wroth, and his countenance fell.*

A. Give an example from your life experiences where you realized you gave, but it may not have been your best offering.

_____
_____
_____
_____
_____
_____
_____

1. How did it make you feel? _____
_____
_____
_____

Study Sheets: Stewardship Characteristics

2. Have you changed and are you giving with a willing heart?

_____
_____
_____

B. 2 Cor. 9:7 *Every man according as he purposeth in his heart, so let him give; not grudgingly, or of necessity: for God loveth a cheerful giver.*

   a. What kind of giver does the Lord love? _____

   b. Man should give as _____ in His heart and not _____ or of _____

C. Jealousy and Selfishness Blocks Your Blessings

In the following, you will notice that the scripture says **look and see**. When you operate in the flesh your sins will block your blessings, and God is still waiting to give you what He promised, in His Covenant to Abraham.

John 4:35 *"Don't you say, 'In four more months the harvest will be here'? I'm telling you to **look and see** that the fields are ready to be harvested, GW.*

2 Tim. 3:1-7 *This know also, that in the last days perilous times shall come. [2] For men shall be lovers of their own selves, covetous, boasters, proud, blasphemers, disobedient to parents, unthankful, unholy, [3] Without natural affection, trucebreakers, false accusers, incontinent, fierce, despisers of those that are good, [4] Traitors, heady, high-minded, lovers of pleasures more than lovers of God; [5] Having a form of godliness, but denying the power thereof: from such turn away. [6] For of this sort are they which creep into houses, and lead captive silly women laden with sins, led away with divers lusts, [7] Ever learning, and never able to come to the knowledge of the truth.*

GOD'S PLAN FOR AN ABUNDANT LIFE: Stewardship, Tithing & Discipleship

Study Sheets:
Stewardship Characteristics

III. Stewards Are Accountable

As you examine your financial status of well being, you must recognize that God has not been slack in His giving to you. You have received an abundant blessing. However, because you are not managing what you have received well, you are failing to be responsible and accountable as a good steward. When you do not recognize and maximize your gifts, you are failing God and delaying what He has stored up for you (Remember, God also allows us to go through trials and tribulations, quickening us into a closer relationship with him).

A. Deut. 14:22 *Thou shalt truly tithe all the increase of thy seed, that the field bringeth forth year by year.*

- What does tithe mean? _____

- What is the seed? _____

- Where is the field that you labor in and who does it belong to?
_____

B. Read the scriptures below, placing yourself in the middle of the discussion about the steward:

Luke 16:1-8: *1And he said also unto his disciples, there was a certain rich man, which had a steward; and the same was accused unto him that he had wasted his goods.*

Have you ever wasted your goods/money/possessions? Yes___ No___

2 And he called him, and said unto him, How is it that I hear this of thee? give an account of thy stewardship; for thou mayest be no longer steward. 3 Then the steward said within himself, What shall I do? for my lord taketh away from me the stewardship: I cannot dig; to beg I am ashamed.

- **Give an account of yourself, be honest, do you pay your tithes or do you tip God?** _____

- What thoughts or excuses came to your mind? _____
_____
_____

Study Sheets:
Stewardship Characteristics

4 I am resolved what to do, that, when I am put out of the stewardship, they may receive me into their houses.

- Who did you turn to when things began to go wrong or terribly bad in your life?
___
___

5 So he called every one of his lord's debtors unto him, and said unto the first, How much owest thou unto my lord? 6 And he said, An hundred measures of oil. And he said unto him, Take thy bill, and sit down quickly, and write fifty. 7 Then said he to another, And how much owest thou? And he said, An hundred measures of wheat. And he said unto him, Take thy bill, and write fourscore. 8 And the lord commended the unjust steward, because he had done wisely: for the children of this world are in their generation wiser than the children of light.

Now that you have read the whole story, do you think God, the Lord is pleased with the steward that was wasteful? Explain

Do you think the unsaved are better at managing their possessions?
___
___

C. Romans 14:12 *So then every one of us shall give account of himself to God.*

Who are you really accountable to and how do you think you measure up to God's will and ways?
___
___

Hebrews 13:17 *Obey them that have the rule over you, and submit yourselves: for they watch for your souls, as they that must give account, that they may do it with joy, and not with grief: for that is unprofitable for you.*

- **Do you have a problem with submission and following the directions of your Pastor, supervisors or people you report to? Explain**
___
___
___

Study Sheets: Stewardship Characteristics

IV. Stewards Serve God and Manage Wealth Wisely:

You are divinely created and wonderfully made for the purpose of managing God's earthly kingdom, for His glory. Wealth is not just monetary gain, for in 3 John 1:2 we learn that God wants you to prosper in wealth, health and in your soul.

> **3 John 1:2** *Beloved, I wish above all things that thou mayest prosper and be in health, even as thy soul prospereth.*

A. Luke 16:9-13 (GW) *{9}{Jesus continued,} "I'm telling you that although wealth is often used in dishonest ways, you should use it to make friends for yourselves. When life is over, you will be welcomed into an eternal home. [10] Whoever can be trusted with very little can also be trusted with a lot. Whoever is dishonest with very little is dishonest with a lot. [11] Therefore, if you can't be trusted with wealth that is often used dishonestly, who will trust you with wealth that is real? [12] If you can't be trusted with someone else's wealth, who will give you your own? [13] "A servant cannot serve two masters. He will hate the first master and love the second, or he will be devoted to the first and despise the second. You cannot serve God and wealth."*

> **Luke 16:9-13 (KJ):** *You Can Not Serve God and Mammon 9 And I say unto you, Make to yourselves friends of the mammon of unrighteousness; that, when ye fail, they may receive you into everlasting habitations. 10 He that is faithful in that which is least is faithful also in much: and he that is unjust in the least is unjust also in much. 11 If therefore ye have not been faithful in the unrighteous mammon, who will commit to your trust the true riches? 12 And if ye have not been faithful in that which is another man's, who shall give you that which is your own? 13 No servant can serve two masters: for either he will hate the one, and love the other; or else he will hold to the one, and despise the other. Ye cannot serve God and mammon.* (KJV)

V. Stewards Have Power To Get Wealth

God has given you power to get wealth but many of you fail to recognize that the real owner of everything that you have belongs to God. If we live according to God's commandments he will bless your and you family forever. **Deut. 28:1-14**

Study Sheets: Stewardship Characteristics

Deut. 8:18 *But remember the Lord your God is the one who makes you wealthy. He's confirming the promise, which he swore to your ancestors. It's still in effect today.*

Proverbs 10:22 *The blessing of the Lord, it maketh rich, and he addeth no sorrow with it.*

Romans 8:17 *And if children, then heirs; heirs of God, and joint-heirs with Christ; if so be that we suffer with him, that we may be also glorified together.*

VI. Stewards Lay Their Treasures In Heaven:

As Stewards of God, you must examine the deeper issues of life to discover what is in your heart, and does it align itself with the truth and righteousness of God. Are you desiring to be rich or do you desire to fulfill the commands of God and to obey His word? Do you reverence the Holiness of God? Do you have a repentant heart and fear the awesome wonder and Power of God?

Matthew 6:19-20 *Lay not up for yourselves treasures upon earth, where moth and rust doth corrupt, and where thieves break through and steal: [20] But lay up for yourselves treasures in heaven, where neither moth nor rust doth corrupt, and where thieves do not break through nor steal:*

Psalm 62:10 *Trust not in oppression, and become not vain in robbery: if riches increase, set not your heart upon them.*

1 Cor. 4:1-2 *Let a man so account of us, as of the ministers of Christ, and stewards of the mysteries of God. [2] Moreover it is required in stewards, that a man be found faithful.*

VII. Stewards Seek The Righteousness of God:

Stewards must know that in all their getting they must have understanding. Godly understanding allows you to understand the ways of God, giving you the knowledge that allows you to flow in the anointing to accomplish God's Plan. Godly wisdom helps you to discern what to seek and how to seek the righteousness of God; that you may be rewarded according to His riches in Christ Jesus. **The righteousness of God requires living a God-centered life.**

Matthew 6:33-34 *But seek ye first the kingdom of God, and his righteousness; and all these things shall be added unto you. [34] Take therefore no thought for the morrow: for the morrow shall take thought for the things of itself. Sufficient unto the day is the evil thereof.*

GOD'S PLAN FOR AN ABUNDANT LIFE: Stewardship, Tithing & Discipleship

Study Sheets:
Stewardship Characteristics

VIII. Stewards Willingly Give:

God does not need your money. The underlying hidden treasures of God set aside for you are directly related to your attitude of giving to God and to others. How do you demonstrate giving of your Time, Talents and Treasures?

Matthew 6:1-4 *Take heed that ye do not your alms before men, to be seen of them: otherwise ye have no reward of your Father which is in heaven. [2] Therefore when thou doest thine alms, do not sound a trumpet before thee, as the hypocrites do in the synagogues and in the streets, that they may have glory of men. Verily I say unto you, They have their reward. [3] But when thou doest alms, let not thy left hand know what thy right hand doeth: [4] That thine alms may be in secret: and thy Father which seeth in secret himself shall reward thee openly.*

Acts 20:33-35 *I have coveted no man's silver, or gold, or apparel. [34] Yea, ye yourselves know, that these hands have ministered unto my necessities, and to them that were with me. [35] I have shewed you all things, how that so laboring ye ought to support the weak, and to remember the words of the Lord Jesus, how he said, It is more blessed to give than to receive.*

Proverbs 3:9 *Honour the Lord with thy substance, and with the firstfruits of all thine increase:*

IX. Stewards Are Faithful & Know How To Pray:

Stewards have a personal and intimate relationship with God based on the amount of time they spend in prayer, fasting, praise, and worship. The giving of your heart, mind, and soul to Christ allows you to commune and abide with God in the Holy of Holies. Your Prayer life can not be centered on just your needs, but, allow God to take you to higher levels of his anointing.

Matthew 6:5-13 *And when thou prayest, thou shalt not be as the hypocrites are: for they love to pray standing in the synagogues and in the corners of the streets, that they may be seen of men. Verily I say unto you, They have their reward. [6] But thou, when thou prayest, enter into thy closet, and when thou hast shut thy door, pray to thy Father which is in secret; and thy Father which seeth in secret shall reward thee openly. [7] But when ye pray, use not vain repetitions, as the heathen do: for they think that they shall be heard for their much speaking. [8] Be not ye therefore like unto them: for your Father knoweth what things ye have need of, before ye ask him. [9] After this manner therefore pray ye: Our Father which art in heaven, Hallowed be thy name. [10] Thy kingdom come. Thy will be done in earth, as it is in heaven. [11] Give*

Study Sheets: Stewardship Characteristics

us this day our daily bread. [12] And forgive us our debts, as we forgive our debtors. [13] And lead us not into temptation, but deliver us from evil: For thine is the kingdom, and the power, and the glory, for ever. Amen.

Stewards pray believing that they have received what they desired .

Mark 11:22-24 *And Jesus answering saith unto them, have faith in God. [23] For verily I say unto you, That whosoever shall say unto this mountain, Be thou removed, and be thou cast into the sea; and shall not doubt in his heart, but shall believe that those things which he saith shall come to pass; he shall have whatsoever he saith. [24] Therefore I say unto you, What things soever ye desire, when ye pray, believe that ye receive them, and ye shall have them.*

James 5:16 *Confess your faults one to another, and pray one for another, that ye may be healed. The effectual fervent prayer of a righteous man availeth much.*

X. Stewards Are Not Hypocrites:

If you fail to accept that you to are robbing God, not repentive of your sins and deceitful, you are a hypocrite. Your tithes and offerings must be given to God with a willing heart, as an outward demonstration of your love for God. Tithes and offering can not be separated. You worship God with your offering, but your tithes are what is due to God.

Matthews 23:23 *"How horrible it will be for you, scribes and Pharisees! You hypocrites! You give {God} one-tenth of your mint, dill, and cumin. But you have neglected justice, mercy, and faithfulness. These are the most important things in Moses' Teachings. You should have done these things without neglecting the others.*

Matthew 23:24-28: *Ye blind guides, which strain at a gnat, and swallow a camel. [25] Woe unto you, scribes and Pharisees, hypocrites! for ye make clean the outside of the cup and of the platter, but within they are full of extortion and excess. [26] Thou blind Pharisee, cleanse first that which is within the cup and platter, that the outside of them may be clean also. [27] Woe unto you, scribes and Pharisees, hypocrites! for ye are like unto whited sepulchres, which indeed appear beautiful outward, but are within full of dead men's bones, and of all uncleanness. [28] Even so ye also outwardly appear righteous unto men, but within ye are full of hypocrisy and iniquity.*

Study Sheets:
Stewardship Characteristics

XI. Faithful Stewards of The Talents:

Stewards of the talents discovered the importance of handling, with excellence, the gifts they receive from God. They also strive to give others opportunities to grow in their work and spiritual relationships with God. God blesses the faithful stewards and servants who are obedient to His Word and those who are doers of the Word. Stewards look beyond the faults of others to see their needs and works to lead that person, or persons closer to our Lord and Savior. Their lives are dedicated to glorifying God with their gifts and talents.

Matthew 25:14-30 *For the kingdom of heaven is as a man traveling into a far country, who called his own servants, and delivered unto them his goods.*

[15] And unto one he gave five talents, to another two, and to another one; to every man according to his several ability; and straightway took his journey. [16] Then he that had received the five talents went and traded with the same, and made them other five talents. [17] And likewise he that had received two, he also gained other two. [18] But he that had received one went and digged in the earth, and hid his lord's money. [19] After a long time the lord of those servants cometh, and reckoneth with them. [20] And so he that had received five talents came and brought other five talents, saying, Lord, thou deliveredst unto me five talents: behold, I have gained beside them five talents more. [21] His lord said unto him, Well done, thou good and faithful servant: thou hast been faithful over a few things, I will make thee ruler over many things: enter thou into the joy of thy lord.

[22] He also that had received two talents came and said, Lord, thou deliveredst unto me two talents: behold, I have gained two other talents beside them. [23] His lord said unto him, Well done, good and faithful servant; thou hast been faithful over a few things, I will make thee ruler over many things: enter thou into the joy of thy lord. [24] Then he which had received the one talent came and said, Lord, I knew thee that thou art an hard man, reaping where thou hast not sown, and gathering where thou hast not strawed: [25] And I was afraid, and went and hid thy talent in the earth: lo, there thou hast that is thine. [26] His lord answered and said unto him, Thou wicked and slothful servant, thou knewest that I reap where I sowed not, and gather where I have not strawed: [27] Thou oughtest therefore to have put my money to the exchangers, and

> *Stewards look beyond the faults of others to see their needs and works to lead that person, or persons closer to our Lord and Savior.*

GOD'S PLAN FOR AN ABUNDANT LIFE: Stewardship, Tithing & Discipleship

Study Sheets:
Stewardship Characteristics

then at my coming I should have received mine own with usury. [28] Take therefore the talent from him, and give it unto him which hath ten talents. [29] For unto every one that hath shall be given, and he shall have abundance: but from him that hath not shall be taken away even that which he hath. [30] And cast ye the unprofitable servant into outer darkness: there shall be weeping and gnashing of teeth.

Matthew 25:31-46 When the Son of man shall come in his glory, and all the holy angels with him, then shall he sit upon the throne of his glory: [32] And before him shall be gathered all nations: and he shall separate them one from another, as a shepherd divideth his sheep from the goats: [33] And he shall set the sheep on his right hand, but the goats on the left. [34] Then shall the King say unto them on his right hand, Come, ye blessed of my Father, inherit the kingdom prepared for you from the foundation of the world: [35] For I was an hungred, and ye gave me meat: I was thirsty, and ye gave me drink: I was a stranger, and ye took me in:

[36] Naked, and ye clothed me: I was sick, and ye visited me: I was in prison, and ye came unto me. [37] Then shall the righteous answer him, saying, Lord, when saw we thee an hungred, and fed thee? or thirsty, and gave thee drink? [38] When saw we thee a stranger, and took thee in? or naked, and clothed thee? [39] Or when saw we thee sick, or in prison, and came unto thee? [40] the King shall answer and say unto them, Verily I say unto you, Inasmuch as ye have done it unto one of the least of these my brethren, ye have done it unto me. [41] Then shall he say also unto them on the left hand, Depart from me, ye cursed, into everlasting fire, prepared for the devil and his angels: [42]

> Verily I say unto you, Inasmuch as ye did it not to one of the least of these, ye did it not to me...

For I was an hungred, and ye gave me no meat: I was thirsty, and ye gave me no drink: [43] I was a stranger, and ye took me not in: naked, and ye clothed me not: sick, and in prison, and ye visited me not. [44] Then shall they also answer him, saying, Lord, when saw we thee an hungred, or athirst, or a stranger, or naked, or sick, or in prison, and did not minister unto thee? [45] Then shall he answer them, saying, Verily I say unto you, Inasmuch as ye did it not to one of the least of these, ye did it not to me. [46] And these shall go away into everlasting punishment: but the righteous into life eternal.

GOD'S PLAN FOR AN ABUNDANT LIFE: Stewardship, Tithing & Discipleship

Study Sheets:
Stewardship Characteristics

XII. Stewards Entrusted With God's Mysteries:

Stewards are given authority and all power (**dunamis power**) as managers of God's creation in this earthly kingdom. We have in us this treasured vessels, which is the power and glory of God through the Holy Spirit that allows us through prayer and the utterance of tongues in the spirit that brings revelation power and quickens one with wisdom, power and understanding. A **steward** who is faithful also enters into the joy of the Lord.

> In Greek, **treasure** is pronounced **thesauros, thay-sow-ros**. A vessel is defined as treasure, wealth, or a deposit. Notice the word sow.

Matthew 25:23 *His lord said unto him, Well done, good and faithful servant; thou hast been faithful over a few things, I will make thee ruler over many things: enter thou into the joy of thy lord.*

2 Cor. 4:7 *But we have this treasure in earthen vessels, that the excellency of the power may be of God, and not of us. For in man according to I John 4:4 Ye are of God, little children, and have overcome them: because greater is he that is in you, than he that is in the world.*

2 Cor. 4:7 *But this precious <u>treasure</u>—this light and power that now shines within us—is held in perishable containers, that is, in our weak bodies. So everyone can see that our glorious power is from God and is not our own.*

1 Cor. 4:1-2: *Let a man so account of us, as of the ministers of Christ, and stewards of the mysteries of God. [2] Moreover it is required in stewards, that a man be found faithful.*

Matthew 13:11 *He answered and said unto them, Because it is given unto you to know the mysteries of the kingdom of heaven, but to them it is not given.*

Luke 8:10 *And he said, Unto you it is given to know the mysteries of the kingdom of God: but to others in parables; that seeing they might not see, and hearing they might not understand.*

1 Cor. 4:1 *Let a man so account of us, as of the ministers of Christ, and stewards of the mysteries of God.*

1 Cor. 13:2 *And though I have the gift of prophecy, and understand all mysteries, and all knowledge; and though I have all faith, so that I could remove mountains, and have not charity, I am nothing.*

1 Cor. 14:2 *For he that speaketh in an unknown tongue speaketh not unto men, but unto God: for no man understandeth him; howbeit in the spirit he speaketh mysteries.*

GOD'S PLAN FOR AN ABUNDANT LIFE: Stewardship, Tithing & Discipleship

Study Sheets:
Stewardship Characteristics

XIII. Stewards of God's House Know When and How To Give and Collect:

1 Corinthians 16:1-3 Now concerning the collection for the saints, as I have given order to the churches of Galatia, even so do ye. [2] Upon the first day of the week let every one of you lay by him in store, as God hath prospered him, that there be no gatherings when I come. [3] And when I come, whomsoever ye shall approve by your letters, them will I send to bring your liberality unto Jerusalem.

Collection By The Stewards:
These two passages, 2 Chron. 24:6, & 9; and I Cor. 16:1-3 give clarity and understanding to the need for Collections in the church. This also sets in place the foundation of the tithes and the Order/direction of how the collection shall be received.

> **Liberality** in Greek translated **haplotes, hap-lot'-ace;** (subjective) sincerity (without dissimulation or self-seeking), or (objective) generosity (copious bestowal: bountifulness, liberal (-ity), simplicity, singleness.
>
> The word **collection** translates into: **logia, log-ee'-ah;** from Greek **logos**: a contribution: collection, and a gathering.

Your tithes and offerings are part of the collection. The collection is giving to God your Tithes and offerings. The collection is for: repair and upkeep of the church, salaries for ministers; the development and or enhancement of ministries for the spreading of the Gospel of Jesus Christ. (Matthew 25:18-20)

> **2 Chron. 24:6** *So the king called for the chief priest Jehoiada and asked him, "Why didn't you require the Levites to bring the contributions from Judah and Jerusalem? The Lord's servant Moses and the assembly had required Israel to give contributions for the use of the tent containing the words of God's promise."* GW

> **2 Chron. 24:6** *So the king called for Jehoiada the High Priest and asked him, "Why haven't you demanded that the Levites go out and collect the Temple taxes from the cities of Judah and from Jerusalem? The tax law enacted by Moses the servant of the Lord must be enforced so that the Temple can be repaired."* KJ

> **2 Chron. 24:9** *And they made a proclamation through Judah and Jerusalem, to bring in to the LORD the collection that Moses the servant of God laid upon Israel in the wilderness.* KJV

GOD'S PLAN FOR AN ABUNDANT LIFE: Stewardship, Tithing & Discipleship

Study Sheets: *Stewardship Characteristics*

1 Cor. 16:1 *Now concerning the <u>collection</u> for the saints, as I have given order to the churches of Galatia, even so do ye.* [2] *Upon the first day of the week let every one of you lay by him in store, as God hath prospered him, that there be no gatherings when I come.* [3] *And when I come, whomsoever ye shall approve by your letters, them will I send to bring your <u>liberality</u> unto Jerusalem. KJV*

Deut. 15:10 *Thou shalt surely give him, and thine heart shall not be grieved when thou givest unto him: because that for this thing the Lord thy God shall bless thee in all thy works, and in all that thou puttest thine hand unto.*

XIV. Stewards Are Not Greedy

Luke 12:16-21: *And he spake a parable unto them, saying, The ground of a certain rich man brought forth plentifully:* [17] *And he thought within himself, saying, What shall I do, because I have no room where to bestow my fruits?* [18] *And he said, This will I do: I will pull down my barns, and build greater; and there will I bestow all my fruits and my goods.* [19] *And I will say to my soul, Soul, thou hast much goods laid up for many years; take thine ease, eat, drink, and be merry.* [20] *But God said unto him, Thou fool, this night thy soul shall be required of thee: then whose shall those things be, which thou hast provided?* [21] *So is he that layeth up treasure for himself, and is not rich toward God.*

XV. Stewards Have Strength & Are Content:

Philip. 4:10-13 *But I rejoiced in the Lord greatly, that now at the last your care of me hath flourished again; wherein ye were also careful, but ye lacked opportunity.* [11] *Not that I speak in respect of want: for I have learned, in whatsoever state I am, therewith to be content.* [12] *I know both how to be abased, and I know how to abound: every where and in all things I am instructed both to be full and to be hungry, both to abound and to suffer need.* [13] *I can do all things through Christ which strengtheneth me.*

GOD'S PLAN FOR AN ABUNDANT LIFE: Stewardship, Tithing & Discipleship

Study Sheets:
Stewardship Characteristics

XVI. Stewards Give Equally With Grace:

1 Peter 4:10 *As every man hath received the gift, even so minister the same one to another, as good stewards of the manifold grace of God.*

2 Cor. 8:1-12 *Moreover, brethren, we do you to wit of the grace of God bestowed on the churches of Macedonia; [2] How that in a great trial of affliction the abundance of their joy and their deep poverty abounded unto the riches of their liberality. [3] For to their power, I bear record, yea, and beyond their power they were willing of themselves; [4] Praying us with much intreaty that we would receive the gift, and take upon us the fellowship of the ministering to the saints. [5] And this they did, not as we hoped, but first gave their own selves to the Lord, and unto us by the will of God. [6] Insomuch that we desired Titus, that as he had begun, so he would also finish in you the same grace also. [7] Therefore, as ye abound in every thing, in faith, and utterance, and knowledge, and in all diligence, and in your love to us, see that ye abound in this grace also. [8] I speak not by commandment, but by occasion of the forwardness of others, and to prove the sincerity of your love. [9] For ye know the grace of our Lord Jesus Christ, that, though he was rich, yet for your sakes he became poor, that ye through his poverty might be rich. [10] And herein I give my advice: for this is expedient for you, who have begun before, not only to do, but also to be forward a year ago. [11] Now therefore perform the doing of it; that as there was a readiness to will, so there may be a performance also out of that which ye have. [12] For if there be first a willing mind, it is accepted according to that a man hath, and not according to that he hath not.*

> *As every man hath received the gift, even so minister the same one to another, as good stewards of the manifold grace of God.*

> *A steward who is faithful also enters into the joy of the Lord.*

2 Cor. 8:13-16 *For I mean not that other men be eased, and ye burdened: [14] But by an equality, that now at this time your abundance may be a supply for their want, that their abundance also may be a supply for your want: that there may be equality: [15] As it is written, He that had gathered much had nothing over; and he that had gathered little had no lack. [16] But thanks be to God, which put the same earnest care into the heart of Titus for you.*

Study Sheets: Stewardship Characteristics

XVII. Stewards Provide for The Church:

1 Cor. 9:1-4; 7-9 *Am I not an apostle? am I not free? have I not seen Jesus Christ our Lord? are not ye my work in the Lord? [2] If I be not an apostle unto others, yet doubtless I am to you: for the seal of mine apostleship are ye in the Lord. [3] Mine answer to them that do examine me is this, [4] Have we not power to eat and to drink?*

[7] Who goeth a warfare any time at his own charges? who planteth a vineyard, and eateth not of the fruit thereof? or who feedeth a flock, and eateth not of the milk of the flock? [8] Say I these things as a man? or saith not the law the same also? [9] For it is written in the law of Moses, Thou shalt not muzzle the mouth of the ox that treadeth out the corn. Doth God take care for oxen?

1 Tim. 5:18 *For the scripture saith, Thou shalt not muzzle the ox that treadeth out the corn. And, The labourer is worthy of his reward.*

Galatians 6:6-10 *Let him that is taught in the word communicate unto him that teacheth in all good things. [7] Be not deceived; God is not mocked: for whatsoever a man soweth, that shall he also reap. [8] For he that soweth to his flesh shall of the flesh reap corruption; but he that soweth to the Spirit shall of the Spirit reap life everlasting. [9] And let us not be weary in well doing: for in due season we shall reap, if we faint not. [10] As we have therefore opportunity, let us do good unto all men, especially unto them who are of the household of faith.*

XVIII. Stewards Know How To Sow

2 Cor. 9:1-15 *For as touching the ministering to the saints, it is superfluous for me to write to you: [2] For I know the forwardness of your mind, for which I boast of you to them of Macedonia, that Achaia was ready a year ago; and your zeal hath provoked very many. [3] Yet have I sent the brethren, lest our boasting of you should be in vain in this behalf; that, as I said, ye may be ready:*

Study Sheets: Stewardship Characteristics

GOD'S PLAN FOR AN ABUNDANT LIFE: Stewardship, Tithing & Discipleship

[4] Lest haply if they of Macedonia come with me, and find you unprepared, we (that we say not, ye) should be ashamed in this same confident boasting. [5] Therefore I thought it necessary to exhort the brethren, that they would go before unto you, and make up beforehand your bounty, whereof ye had notice before, that the same might be ready, as a matter of bounty, and not as of covetousness. [6] But this I say, He which soweth sparingly shall reap also sparingly; and he which soweth bountifully shall reap also bountifully. [7] Every man according as he purposeth in his heart, so let him give; not grudgingly, or of necessity: for God loveth a cheerful giver. [8] And God is able to make all grace abound toward you; that ye, always having all sufficiency in all things, may abound to every good work:

[9] (As it is written, He hath dispersed abroad; he hath given to the poor: his righteousness remaineth for ever. [10] Now he that ministereth seed to the sower both minister bread for your food, and multiply your seed sown, and increase the fruits of your righteousness;) [11] Being enriched in every thing to all bountifulness, which causeth through us thanksgiving to God.

> *Now he that ministereth seed to the sower both minister bread for your food, and multiply your seed sown, and increase the fruits of your righteousness...*

[12] For the administration of this service not only supplieth the want of the saints, but is abundant also by many thanksgivings unto God; [13] Whiles by the experiment of this ministration they glorify God for your professed subjection into the gospel of Christ, and for your liberal distribution unto them, and unto all men; [14] And by their prayer for you, which long after you for the exceeding grace of God in you. [15] Thanks be unto God for his unspeakable gift.

Study Sheets: Stewardship Characteristics

XIX. Stewards Are Not Deceitful:

Acts 5:1-11 *But a certain man named Ananias, with Sapphira his wife, sold a possession, [2] And kept back part of the price, his wife also being privy to it, and brought a certain part, and laid it at the apostles' feet. [3] But Peter said, Ananias, why hath Satan filled thine heart to lie to the Holy Ghost, and to keep back part of the price of the land? [4] Whiles it remained, was it not thine own? and after it was sold, was it not in thine own power? why hast thou conceived this thing in thine heart? thou hast not lied unto men, but unto God. [5] And Ananias hearing these words fell down, and gave up the ghost: and great fear came on all them that heard these things. [6] And the young men arose, wound him up, and carried him out, and buried him. [7] And it was about the space of three hours after, when his wife, not knowing what was done, came in. [8] And Peter answered unto her, Tell me whether ye sold the land for so much? And she said, Yea, for so much. [9] Then Peter said unto her, How is it that ye have agreed together to tempt the Spirit of the Lord? behold, the feet of them which have buried thy husband are at the door, and shall carry thee out. [10] Then fell she down straightway at his feet, and yielded up the ghost: and the young men came in, and found her dead, and, carrying her forth, buried her by her husband. [11] And great fear came upon all the church, and upon as many as heard these things.*

XX. Stewards Are Transformed:

Romans 12:1-2 *I beseech you therefore, brethren, by the mercies of God, that ye present your bodies a living sacrifice, holy, acceptable unto God, which is your reasonable service. [2] And be not conformed to this world: but be ye transformed by the renewing of your mind, that ye may prove what is that good, and acceptable, and perfect, will of God.*

Romans 8:27-32 *And he that searcheth the hearts knoweth what is the mind of the Spirit, because he maketh intercession for the saints according to the will of God. [28] And we know that all things work together for good to them that love God, to them who are the called according to his purpose. [29] For whom he did foreknow, he also did predestinate to be conformed to the image of his Son, that he might be the firstborn among many brethren. [30] Moreover whom he did predestinate, them he also called: and whom he called, them he also justified: and whom he justified, them he also glorified.*

James Strong, New Strong's dictionary of Hebrew and Greek words [computer file], electronic ed., Logos Library System, (Nashville: Thomas Nelson) 1997, c1996.
The King James Version, (Cambridge: Cambridge) 1769.
The King James Version, (Cambridge: Cambridge) 1769.
God's Plan for An Abundant Life: Stewardship, Tithing & Discipleship

Notes

GOD'S PLAN FOR AN ABUNDANT LIFE: Stewardship, Tithing & Discipleship

GOD'S PLAN FOR AN ABUNDANT LIFE: Stewardship, Tithing & Discipleship

Notes

GOD'S PLAN FOR AN ABUNDANT LIFE: Stewardship, Tithing & Discipleship

Seminar 2

Worship God By Giving Your Tithes & Offerings

Evangelist Anton L. Seals, Sr.
VASTT Ministry

GOD'S PLAN FOR AN ABUNDANT LIFE: Stewardship, Tithing & Discipleship

Outline of Seminar 2
Worship God By Giving: Tithes & Offerings

Introduction, Purpose & Mission	53-56
Managing God's Wealth	51
God's Way Versus Our Ways	52
Historical Relationship of Tithing	53
Tithing History	54-58
Group Activity I: (1-9): What God Said About Tithing	59-67
Group Activity II: The Three T's	68
Bible Truths	69
R U Factors	70
Tithes and Offerings (A Covenant Commitment With God)	71-72
Key Factors That Help To Develop A Life of Tithing	73-74
Group Activity III: God's Plan for A Spirit Filled Life: (Stewardship & Discipleship)	75-81
It Is Not What It Looks Like: Believe and Operate In Faith	82
Principles of Giving	83
Why The Church Must Teach Giving	84
Why Give To God?	85
Difference Between Fund-Raisers & Tithing	85-88
God Wants Your Best Sacrificial Offering	88
Giving Your Tithes and Offering	89-90
Sowing and Reaping Your Abundant Harvest	91-95
How Can The People Hear Without A Pastor?	96-97
You Must Trust God and The God In Your Pastor	98-99
Giving With A Willing Heart	100-106

GOD'S PLAN FOR AN ABUNDANT LIFE: Stewardship, Tithing & Discipleship

Introduction

The training that you are embarking upon has been developed for the sole purpose of assisting your Pastor(s) to water the seeds that have been planted for both your spiritual growth and the Corporate Body of Christ. It is our goal to richly enhance the level of commitment of church leaders, the congregation, and those who Love the Lord with all of their hearts, minds, and souls to give with willing hearts their tithes and offerings. We pray that the Light of God be seen in your obedience to live according to the Word of God. If you truly love the Lord there will be a tremendous transformation of how you willingly give to God your:

- **TIME: to Serve**
- **TALENTS: Discovering and using your spiritual gifts for His Glory**
- **TREASURES: giving of your money through your tithes and offerings**

A life of **Giving** back to God is the art of mastering the duty of Stewardship. Can you believe that God loves us? He loves us so much that he has given a **Trust** to us with sole responsibility of managing the Kingdom on earth. How can we enter the gates of heaven if we fail to take care of the gifts he bestowed, endowed, and willed to us? Stewardship, Tithing, and Discipleship are a walk of faith. We must believe in the righteousness and truth of God's Word.

We can never beat God's Giving, for He does not need your money, the Cattle on a Thousand Hills is mine said the Lord. However, He does Command that a tenth of your gross income be brought with a willing heart to **His Storehouse, the Church**. We must come to understand that giving our tithes and offerings is a part of praise and worship service. You must never stop giving your best for the Lord. You are called to serve at a higher level of excellence. There is a shift in your relationship with Christ Jesus, and your transformation has made you a new creature in Christ. The old man died and you have received the refreshing that destroys the old mind that finds old lame excuses to justify why and how you rob God.

> **Discover your Treasures in your Earthen Vessel and allow God, through His Son Jesus Christ, to release the Abundant Blessings laid up in Heaven for true believers.**

Discover your Treasures in your Earthen Vessel and allow God, through His Son Jesus Christ, to release the Abundant Blessings laid up in Heaven for true believers. He holds keys that open treasures stored from His Warehouse, called Blessed Assurance. If Sons of God, then you are Heirs to the Kingdom of God, and where God is there is peace, joy, happiness, love, and His Riches in Glory. Remember, He is the Owner and you are the proprietor, manager, which have been given Divine Stewardship to Manage, with Wisdom, what He has blessed you with. It all belongs to God.

GOD'S PLAN FOR AN ABUNDANT LIFE: Stewardship, Tithing & Discipleship

Introduction

Purpose of Seminar:

The primary focus of this training seminar is to provide a holistic approach for training the church leadership and congregation according to what God says about giving your tithes, offerings, and the giving of your Time, Talents, and Treasures. The training includes instructions on the invaluable elements of:

1. Stewardship
   a. The Divine Creation of Man: As Stewards(ship)
   b. Stewards Over What God Has Given To You
   c. Stewards of God Earthly Kingdom
   d. Seek Ye First The Kingdom Of God and His Righteous

2. Tithes
   a. Ownership of God
   b. Paying your Tithes and Offerings
   c. Sowing and Harvesting

3. Discipleship
   a. Living According To God's Word
   b. Becoming a Living Epistle
   c. A Servant's Heart (Bondservant)

Mission:

The mission is to teach what God promised his people concerning His Divine Covenant with Abraham and the seed of Abraham. God promised:

Genesis 12:2-3 *And I will make of thee a great nation, and I will bless thee, and make thy name great; and thou shalt be a blessing: [3] And I will bless them that bless thee, and curse him that curseth thee: and in thee shall all families of the earth be blessed.*

Acts 3:25 *"It is you who are the sons of the prophets, and of the covenant which God made with your fathers, saying to Abraham, 'And in your seed all the families of the earth shall be blessed.''*

Malachi 3:10 *Bring ye all the tithes into the storehouse, that there may be meat in mine house, and prove me now herewith, saith the Lord of hosts, if I will not open you the windows of heaven, and pour you out a blessing, that there shall not be room enough to receive it.*

GOD'S PLAN FOR AN ABUNDANT LIFE: Stewardship, Tithing & Discipleship

Introduction

Luke 6:38 *Give, and it shall be given unto you; good measure, pressed down, and shaken together, and running over, shall men give into your bosom. For with the same measure that ye mete withal it shall be measured to you again.*

Bible Truths: To Manage God's Wealth You Must Be Transformed

Rom 12: 1-2 *1. I beseech you therefore, brethren, by the mercies of God, that ye present your bodies a living sacrifice, Holy, acceptable unto God, which is your reasonable service. 2. And be not conformed to this world: but be ye transformed by the renewing of your mind, that ye may prove what is that good, and acceptable, and perfect, will of God.*

Table Discussions:
- Do you need to be transformed? Or just the non-believers and sinners?
- What do you need to do to be transformed?

2 Tim 3:16-17 *All scripture is given by inspiration of God, and is profitable for doctrine, for reproof, for correction, for instruction in righteousness: [17] That the man of God may be perfect, thoroughly furnished unto all good works.*

Stewardship and Tithing is a Spiritual Endowment in Christ that destroys the desires of the flesh and materialism. These are lustful desires that are warring against the will of God, concerning us.

STOP

Reflect and be honest with yourself:
How much of your time is spent thinking of God or the things pleasing to God?
_____
_____

Make a list of things you thought about in the past 48 hours?
_____
_____

Copyright © 2002 VASTT Ministry & Publishing

Introduction

GOD'S WAY — YOUR WAY
EXAMINE YOUR THOUGHTS CAREFULLY

- (Do you live by circumstances or by principles)

CREATE NEW THOUGHTS WHICH CONFORM TO GOD'S TRUTHS and RIGHTEOUSNESS

MAT. 6:33   **Truth and Righteousness**
"But seek first His kingdom and His righteousness; and all these things shall be added to you."

2COR 10:4-5   **Obedience**
For the weapons of our warfare are not carnal, but mighty through God to the pulling down of strong holds;) [5] Casting down imaginations, and every high thing that exalteth itself against the knowledge of God, and bringing into captivity every thought to the obedience of Christ;

DOES MY THINKING LINE UP WITH GOD'S TRUTH?

- HEB. 4:12   The Word of God is Quick and Powerful

- 2 TIM 3:16-17   All Scripture is Given by Inspiration of God

- 2 COR 5:15   All Things Are for Your Sake

- Acts 20:35   It Is More Blessed To Give Than To Receive

CHANGE YOUR THINKING!!!

GOD'S PLAN FOR AN ABUNDANT LIFE: Stewardship, Tithing & Discipleship

Tithing History

Historical Relationship of Tithing

MELCHIZEDEK [mel KIZ eh deck] (king of righteousness) - A king of Salem (Jerusalem) and priest of the Most High God, see the following scriptures: Gen. 14:17-20; Ps. 110:4; Heb. 5:6-11; 6:20-7:28). Melchizedek's appearance and disappearance in the Book of Genesis is a move of the Spirit of God and is seen in our carnal mind as mysterious events. Melchizedek and Abraham first met after Abraham's defeat of Chedorlaomer and his three allies. Abraham saw Melchizedek as a symbol of the High Priest, as in Jesus Christ, whom he gave a tithe.

> The practice of giving a tenth of income or property extends into Hebrew history before the time of the Mosaic Law.

Melchizedek presented bread and wine to Abraham and his weary men, *demonstrating friendship and religious kinship*. He bestowed a blessing on Abraham in the name of El Elyon ("God Most High"), and praised God for giving Abraham a victory in battle (Gen. 14:17-20). The fact of the matter is that the word tithe never appears in scriptures prior to Gen. 14:17-20. Another key factor of importance is that God mentions giving tithes, a command given to mankind by God before the writing of the Ten Commandments, the book of Laws, long before the area of Leviticus.

Abraham presented Melchizedek with a tithe (a tenth) of all the booty he had gathered. **By this act, Abraham indicated that he recognized Melchizedek as a fellow-worshiper of the one true God**, as well as a priest, who ranked higher spiritually than himself. Melchizedek's existence shows that there were people other than Abraham and his family who served the true God.

The practice of giving a tenth of one's income or property is an offering to God. The custom of paying a tithe was an ancient tradition found among many nations of the ancient world. The practice of giving a tenth of income or property extends into Hebrew history before the time of the Mosaic Law. The first recorded instance of tithing in the Bible occurs in Genesis 14:17-20.

The law of Moses prescribed tithing in some detail. Leviticus 27:30-32 stated that the tithe of

Tithing History

TITHE

In the Old Testament the purpose of the giving of a tenth was, to meet the material needs of the Levite, the stranger, the fatherless (the orphan), and the widow (Deut. 26:12-13). The tithe was an expression of gratitude to God by His people. Basic to tithing was the acknowledgment of God's ownership of everything in the earth.

In the New Testament the words "tithe" and "tithing" appear only eight times: (Matt. 23:23; Luke 11:42; 18:12; Heb. 7:1-10).

Matthew 23:23-26 *Woe unto you, scribes and Pharisees, hypocrites! for ye pay **tithe** of mint and anise and cummin, and have omitted the weightier matters of the law, judgment, mercy, and faith: these ought ye to have done, and not to leave the other undone. [24] Ye blind guides, which strain at a gnat, and swallow a camel. [25] Woe unto you, scribes and Pharisees, hypocrites! for ye make clean the outside of the cup and of the platter, but within they are full of extortion and excess. [26] Thou blind Pharisee, cleanse first that which is within the cup and platter, that the outside of them may be clean also.*

Luke 11:40-45 *Ye fools, did not he that made that which is without make that which is within also? [41] But rather give alms of such things as ye have; and, behold, all things are clean unto you. [42] But woe unto you, Pharisees! for ye **tithe** mint and rue and all manner of herbs, and pass over judgment and the love of God: these ought ye to have done, and not to leave the other undone. [43] Woe unto you, Pharisees! for ye love the uppermost seats in the synagogues, and greetings in the markets. [44] Woe unto you, scribes and Pharisees, hypocrites! for ye are as graves which appear not, and the men that walk over them are not aware of them. [45] Then answered one of the lawyers, and said unto him, Master, thus saying thou reproachest us also.*

Luke 18:10-14 *Two men went up into the temple to pray; the one a Pharisee, and the other a publican. [11] The Pharisee stood and prayed thus with himself, God, I thank thee, that I am not as other men are, extortioners, unjust, adulterers, or even as this publican. [12] I fast twice in the week, I give **tithes** of all that I possess. [13] And the publican, standing afar off, would not lift up so much as his eyes unto heaven, but smote upon his breast, saying, God be merciful to me a sinner. [14] I tell you, this man went down to his house justified rather than the other: for every one that exalteth himself shall be abased; and he that humbleth himself shall be exalted.*

Hebrews 7:1-10 *For this Melchisedec, king of Salem, priest of the most high God, who met Abraham returning from the slaughter of the kings, and blessed him; [2] To whom also Abraham **gave a tenth part of all**; first being by interpretation King of righteousness, and after that also King of Salem, which is, King of peace; [3] Without father, without mother, without descent, having neither beginning of days, nor end of life; but made like unto the*

GOD'S PLAN FOR AN ABUNDANT LIFE: Stewardship, Tithing & Discipleship

Tithing History

*Son of God; abideth a priest continually. [4] Now consider how great this man was, unto whom even the patriarch Abraham gave the tenth of the spoils. [5] And verily they that are of the sons of Levi, who receive the office of the priesthood, have a commandment to take **tithes** of the people according to the law, that is, of their brethren, though they come out of the loins of Abraham: [6] But he whose descent is not counted from them received **tithes** of Abraham, and blessed him that had the promises. [7] And without all contradiction the less is blessed of the better. [8] And here men that die receive **tithes**; but there he receiveth them, of whom it is witnessed that he liveth. [9] And as I may so say, Levi also, who receiveth **tithes**, payed **tithes** in Abraham. [10] For he was yet in the loins of his father, when Melchisedec met him.*

> *And as I may so say, Levi also, who receiveth tithes, payed tithes in Abraham. For he was yet in the loins of his father, when Melchisedec met him.*

Giving should be systematic and by no means limited to a tithe of our incomes but should and must include giving of our offering and giving of our time, talents and treasures. We recognize that all we have is from God. **We are called to be faithful Stewards of all our possessions, (Rom. 14:12; 1 Cor. 9:3-14; 16:1-3; 2 Cor. 8:9).** See the Chapter on Stewards Are God's Anointed Managers.

God's Ownership is one of the Key Factors in understanding the Principle of Giving and returning to God a minimum of a tenth of your earnings.

Tithes as defined in Hebrew has several meanings: (Strong's Concordance)

- **Ashar (aw-shar)**; Properly to *accumulate*

- Chiefly (specific) to grow, *causative make rich*: To become or make rich, (asar).

- **Asar, (awsar)** comes from the primitive root word that is identical with (Ashar). To accumulate; but used only as denominative in Hebrew: meaning (eser); to tithe. **To take or give a tenth: surely, give (take) the tenth, (have, take) tithe or tithing**

- In Greek the word tithe means to apodekatoo, (ap-od-ek-at-o'-o) from Greek words meaning Apo and dekatoo; meaning to tithe (as debtor or creditor), (give, pay. Take) **tithe.**

We are debtors to and in Christ Jesus, who died on Calvary, He paid the debt in full for our sins. When Jesus died for us, His blood was a ransom that reconciles us back to God. We are cleansed and sanctified by His blood through the Lord God our Father, who gave his only begotten Son for our sakes.

GOD'S PLAN FOR AN ABUNDANT LIFE: Stewardship, Tithing & Discipleship

Tithing History

God created you and made me/you/us Stewards of a sacred trust that we are blessed to have. Not only are tithe mentioned in the Old Testament but in the New Testament, **Matthew 25:14,** there is a parable that says: *"For the kingdom of heaven is as a man travelling into a far country, who called his own servants, and delivered unto them his goods."* What have you done with your talents given you?

Tithing, similar to the principles of Discipleship and Stewardship, must be taught systematically in all ministries as directed by the pastor, his/her ministerial staff and lay leaders. **Tithing** will not grow without teaching biblical and spiritual principles. Church growth is in direct correlation with the expansion of teaching and Christian Education.

- **A giving church is a *teaching* church**
- **A *reaching* church teaches the developmental principles of evangelism**
- **A *teaching* church develops and multiplies Disciples for Discipleship and strong Leaders who are Christ Centered**

Paying *tithes* and giving your offerings is part of the worship service. It is a sacred act that involves ones internal level of faith and is manifested, on Sundays, as an outward expression of your trust and reverence to the sovereign power and grace of God. In most churches, tithes and offerings are collected as part of the worship service or immediately following praise and worship. Tithing is a command given to us by God.

> **Giving God your tithes and offering must be of a free will that is in your heart. It must not be given grudgingly.**

Giving God your tithes and offering must be of a free will that is in your heart. It must not be given grudgingly. Giving your tithes is what is due. You can not pay God. He is the Creator and Owner of all things, who also has Sovereign Power. Your Sacrificial Offering, which releases your Blessing should be Above and Beyond your tithes. *It is your offering that brings 30, 60, and 100 fold returns.* There should be an excitement about Blessing God for all He is doing for you, both seen and unseen. Your giving and paying tithes should flow as though it is rushing water excited by the willingness to bless someone's desert thirst. The laws of giving and reaping are contrary to man's normal thinking process. The Word says you must Give to Get. It is better to give than to receive.

The mature Christian understands that the Lord is the Owner and everything we have is a gift from God. You can never beat God Giving. God has a Divine Master Plan for His believers, and they shall never want if they subscribe to his lifetime membership of prosperity and blessings. It is called God's Plan for an Abundant Life. It is God's will for us to inherit the Kingdom of God, because we are the sons, and heirs of God's earthly kingdom.

GOD'S PLAN FOR AN ABUNDANT LIFE: Stewardship, Tithing & Discipleship

Tithing History

God's Plan For An Abundant Life is the only financial/banking system plan, investment plan, IRA, 401K or any kind of stock venture deals that gives you a 100% (per cent) investment without you first giving to Him. God always gives us more than we deserve. His unlimited grace, manifested in the form of His Favor in our lives, yields countless blessings. For the progressive believers, if you want or need to say investment, your increase is beyond anything you can ask or dare to think, if you follow God's Laws of Abundance, found in the Word of God. God's Plan is better than any investment plan or credit card, and more dependable than existing systems for emergency assistance, health care services, employment, housing, training, counseling, healing, deliverance, breakthrough strategies and quick fixes. Not only do you get Blessed Services, you/we are receiving it all the time, with compassion, Grace, and Mercy. The Blessings Never End When You Obey the Will and Commands of God. Your giving to God is greater than investments and His blessing are everlasting and not dependent on others. It is based on your personal but intimate relationship with God, who is our Father (Abba).

When you tithe your inner spirit is being released to link up with God in the heavens. This linking transcends the ability of your mind to comprehend what God is doing and why you are being blessed. The Lord's Blessings come even when I/you/we know we did not and do not deserve the increase and benefits of God. In the Spiritual realm we call these blessing God's Riches In Glory. God delivers back to you a portion of your inheritance as promised in His Covenant with Abraham. He said I will bless the seed of the seed. "I do not know about you but I decree that I am a Seed of Abraham." I hope you are ready to claim your position of authority and relationship with our Father in Heaven. He releases through the angels manifold blessings to you. You never have to go to a bank, just put your tithes and offering in the Storehouse. He will Bless you and your family and those you are praying for. He will hear your cry for the non-believers. If you are faithful in your intercessory prayers, He will hear your cries and will respond by drawing and welcoming new converts into His investment program called the Plan of Salvation, Sanctification, and Eternal Glory.

Through the Power of the Holy Ghost he will fix loneliness, divorce, anger, depression, doubt and fears. He will make a way out of no way, and destroy the spirit of lack, lust, vanity, selfishness, and adultery. There is so much more (You may list some items that speak to what He has done for you and yours, and others). This type of Plan is Spiritual and only those that know and have a relationship with the Master, Owner, and Chief Operating Officer of all the riches in Glory in the earth and in Heaven, understand the parables of God.

> **Your giving to God is greater than investments and His blessings are everlasting and not dependent on others. It is based on your personal but intimate relationship with God, who is our Father (Abba).**

GOD'S PLAN FOR AN ABUNDANT LIFE: Stewardship, Tithing & Discipleship

Tithing History

To those who for years have been faithful to ministries but failed to pay tithes and give offerings, you are like unto the seeds that fall on stony ground. It is your seed that is choking the seeds of the new Christians who are seeking to be more than pew holders. They desire to be doers and to know the voice of the Shepard. What's your agenda and how do you witness for Christ when your storehouse account is in the red? Why do you rob God when you were created to be the Stewards over the Warehouse?

You represent the wolves who are Holy Ghost filled, they shout praises, but they will not commit to the higher callings of Christ. They seek excellence but are not willing to surrender their all to Christ.

> When we teach of God's Word we receive faith to believe and to become free in the spiritual and physical realms. Faith comes by hearing the Word of God.

These are basic principals of Discipleship, Tithing, and Stewardship and must become through biblical references, and testimonials, a part of the church's regular focus, preached from the pulpit, and taught in the board room and in every ministry. The willing souls who learn God's truth and lives according to His Word, will experience greater peace. They have the Blessed Assurance, in Jesus. When you teach tithing, stewardship, and discipleship, you are teaching spiritual development at the highest level. When we teach of God's Word we receive faith to believe and to become free in the spiritual and physical realms. Faith comes by hearing the Word of God.

Romans 8:1-6 *So those who are believers in Christ Jesus can no longer be condemned. The standards of the Spirit, who gives life through Christ Jesus, have set you free from the standards of sin and death. It is impossible to do what God's standards demand, because of the weakness our human nature has. But God sent his Son to have a human nature as sinners have and to pay for sin. That way God condemned sin in our corrupt nature. Therefore, we, who do not live by our corrupt nature but by our spiritual nature, are able to meet God's standards. Those who live by the corrupt nature have the corrupt nature's attitude. But those who live by the spiritual nature have the spiritual nature's attitude. The corrupt nature's attitude leads to death. But the spiritual nature's attitude leads to life and peace.*

GOD'S PLAN FOR AN ABUNDANT LIFE: Stewardship, Tithing & Discipleship

Group Activity 1

What God Said About Tithing
Tithe Scriptures

Group Instructions:
Read the following comments and scriptures. Discuss and list the answers that reflect the feelings and understanding of your group. Note, this is not an exercise of right or wrong. This exercise is to help you get the Word of God concerning tithes deep into you belly forever more.

1. Why does God tell us that the tithe, whether of the seed or of the fruit, is Holy unto him, but we fail to give our tithes and offering?

> **Leviticus 27:30; 32** *and all the **tithe** of the land, whether of the seed of the land, or of the fruit of the tree, is the Lord's: it is holy unto the Lord. (32) And concerning the **tithe** of the herd, or of the flock, even of whatsoever passeth under the rod, the tenth shall be holy unto the Lord.*

God's Word teaches us in:
   Luke 8:11: *Now the parable is this:* <u>**The seed is the Word of God.**</u>

If we are not hearers and doers of God's Word then our seed within us will be trodden down, wither away and take no root.

A Tither is a Steward who must therefore be a sower of God's seed, but only if we can hear God and the seed takes root deep down inside of us. **Read Luke 8:4-18**

Write Your Comments: _____

_____
_____
_____
_____

GOD'S PLAN FOR AN ABUNDANT LIFE: Stewardship, Tithing & Discipleship

Group Activity 1

2. Read Numbers 18:26-32.

Discuss in your group the importance of the tithes given to the Levites. Notice how the Lord commanded Moses to have tithes collected with a special offering given to God and to Aaron from the tithes. This special offering is called a heave offering or sacrificial offerings that are consecrated as the best of the best. **What is God saying to his people about giving their tithes?**

Thus speak unto the Levites, and say unto them, When ye take of the children of Israel the **tithes** which I have given you from them for your inheritance, then ye shall offer up an **heave** offering of it for the Lord, even a tenth part of the tithe. And this your **heave** offering shall be reckoned unto you, as though it were the corn of the threshingfloor, and as the fullness of the winepress.

> **A heave pronounced teruwmah, ter-oo-maw'offering,** *is an offering, or present, a sacrifice (Deut. 12:11). This tells us that we are to give the Priest, Aaron, a present or an offering as a sacrifice from within the tithes. This is a tithe of the tithe.*

In the New Testament this would refer to the house of God the place of worship where you are to bring your tithes to the Pastor, Shepard, the priest of God's house.

3. In this exercise read Malachi 3:7-12.

> *[7] Even from the days of your fathers ye are gone away from mine ordinances, and have not kept them. Return unto me, and I will return unto you, saith the Lord of hosts. But ye said, Wherein shall we return?*

Starting in the 7th verse what did God say he will do if we return unto him? _____ Can you expect the blessing of God to be upon your life if your are not living according to His ordinances?

> *[8] Will a man rob God? Yet ye have robbed me. But ye say, Wherein have we robbed thee? In tithes and offerings.*

How do we rob God? _____

_____

> *[9] Ye are cursed with a curse: for ye have robbed me, even this whole nation.*

GOD'S PLAN FOR AN ABUNDANT LIFE: Stewardship, Tithing & Discipleship

Group Activity 1

Who is cursed with a curse? _____

Explain: _____
_____
_____

> [10] Bring ye all the tithes into the storehouse, that there may be meat in mine house, and prove me now herewith, saith the Lord of hosts, if I will not open you the windows of heaven, and pour you out a blessing, that there shall not be room enough to receive it.

What are we to bring to the storehouse? _____

What will be in your house if you bring your tithes to God's storehouse? _____

What does God mean by prove me? _____
_____

How can you help others to understand or imagine what it would be like to have God pouring out blessings that there will not be room enough to receive it?

Explain: _____
_____
_____

> [11] And I will rebuke the devourer for your sakes, and he shall not destroy the fruits of your ground; neither shall your vine cast her fruit before the time in the field, saith the Lord of hosts. [12] And all nations shall call you blessed: for ye shall be a delightsome land, saith the Lord of hosts.

4. Answer the questions listed below and discuss in your group what God says about tithes and explain why you feel you do not give tithes and offerings. **Are you a hypocrite?** _____. You know the Word of God, yet you fail to give your tithes and offerings.

GOD'S PLAN FOR AN ABUNDANT LIFE: Stewardship, Tithing & Discipleship

Group Activity 1

Matthew 23:23-25 *Woe unto you, scribes and Pharisees, hypocrites! for ye pay tithe of mint and anise and cummin, and have omitted the weightier matters of the law, judgment, mercy, and faith: these ought ye to have done, and not to leave the other undone. [24] Ye blind guides, which strain at a gnat, and swallow a camel. [25] Woe unto you, scribes and Pharisees, hypocrites! for ye make clean the outside of the cup and of the platter, but within they are full of extortion and excess.*

In Matthew 23:23-25 this chapter and verse are written in red denoting that Jesus is speaking directly to the religious leaders of those days. Since the Word of God is the same today as it was yesterday, should we honor God's saying today? If yes, then all of us, especially church leaders, must set an example by giving their tithes and offerings. Are you a Tither? _____

In Luke 21:1-4 *And he looked up, and saw the rich men casting their gifts into the treasury. [2] And he saw also a certain poor widow casting in thither two mites. [3] And he said, Of a truth I say unto you, that this poor widow hath cast in more than they all: [4] For all these have of their abundance cast in unto the offerings of God: but she of her penury hath cast in all the living that she had.*

Why was God more pleased by the poor widows offering rather than the rich rulers offerings? Explain: _____
_____
_____

5. Hebrews 7:1-13 (See Gen. 14:18-24)

For this Melchisedec, king of Salem, priest of the most high God, who met Abraham returning from the slaughter of the kings, and blessed him; [2] To whom also Abraham gave a tenth part of all; first being by interpretation King of righteousness, and after that also King of Salem, which is, King of peace; [3] Without father, without mother, without descent, having neither beginning of days, nor end of life; but made like unto the Son of God; abideth a priest continually. [4] Now consider how great this man was, unto whom even the patriarch Abraham gave the tenth of the spoils.

GOD'S PLAN FOR AN ABUNDANT LIFE: Stewardship, Tithing & Discipleship

Group Activity 1

Read verses 3 and 4. Abraham's giving to Melchisedic is an example of giving to (the) _____ If Abraham the patriarch gave a tithe then why would you or others not want to give your tithes and offering?

Explain: _____

_____

_____

> *[5] And verily they that are of the sons of Levi, who receive the office of the priesthood, have a commandment to take tithes of the people according to the law, that is, of their brethren, though they come out of the loins of Abraham: [6] But he whose descent is not counted from them received tithes of Abraham, and blessed him that had the promises. [7] And without all contradiction the less is blessed of the better.*

While we are made a little lower than the angels we are always the lesser in the face of God. Therefore, we should humble ourselves, as our father Abraham did, and give our tithes and offerings as we worship Jesus the Son of the Living God.

> *[8] And here men that die receive tithes; but there he receiveth them, of whom it is witnessed that he liveth. [9] And as I may so say, Levi also, who receiveth tithes, payed tithes in Abraham. [10] For he was yet in the loins of his father, when Melchisedec met him.*

The laws of the Levitical period had not been written, yet we see here another example of the prophetic Word of God being manifested by the giving of tithes to be a blessing for the Levites.

These verses speak volumes to believers who believe in the Word that we are heirs and the blessed, the called, the chosen, and the peculiar people of God.

Giving your tithes and offerings with a willing heart fulfills God's covenant to bless the seed of Abraham. When you bless the Lord with your tithes and offerings you are blessing your seed, the seed of the unborn in the loins of your families yet born.

> *[11] If therefore perfection were by the Levitical priesthood, (for under it the people received the law), what further need was there that another priest should rise after the order of Melchisedec, and not be called after the order of Aaron? [12] For the priesthood being changed, there is made of necessity a change also of the law. [13] For he of whom these things are spoken pertaineth to another tribe, of which no man gave attendance at the altar.*

GOD'S PLAN FOR AN ABUNDANT LIFE: Stewardship, Tithing & Discipleship

Group Activity 1

Tithes and offerings are not given to men, nor to priest, shepherds, pastors or overseers, but to God through his Son Jesus Christ. These are God's appointed vessels chosen by God to be blessed to do the will of God and for the spreading of the Gospel of Jesus Christ. These individuals are not the judge of your souls.

We are also reminded not to bring offerings to God with ought in our hearts. We need to repent and seek forgiveness for our sins with God and others.

> **Matthew 5:23-24** *Therefore if thou bring thy gift to the altar, and there rememberest that thy brother hath ought against thee; [24] Leave there thy gift before the altar, and go thy way; first be reconciled to thy brother, and then come and offer thy gift.*

> **Mark 11:25** *And when ye stand praying, forgive, if ye have ought against any: that your Father also which is in heaven may forgive you your trespasses.*

6. In I Corth. 9:11-14   Paul Teaches The Right to Live On The Gospel:

After reading these scriptures discuss in your groups what these scriptures mean to you and list the responses of your group. How can these scriptures help to improve the level of giving tithes and offerings in your ministry groups, and within the congregation?

> **In I Corth. 9:11-14** *Who goeth a warfare any time at his own charges? who planteth a vineyard, and eateth not of the fruit thereof? or who feedeth a flock, and eateth not of the milk of the flock? [8] Say I these things as a man? or saith not the law the same also? [9] For it is written in the law of Moses, Thou shalt not muzzle the mouth of the ox that treadeth out the corn. Doth God take care for oxen? [10] Or saith he it altogether for our sakes? For our sakes, no doubt, this is written: that he that ploweth should plow in hope; and that he that thresheth in hope should be partaker of his hope. [11] If we have sown unto you spiritual things, is it a great thing if we shall reap your carnal things? [12] If others be partakers of this power over you, are not we rather? Nevertheless we have not used this power; but suffer all things, lest we should hinder the gospel of Christ.*

Paul teaches the church that it is right in the sight of God that ministers and apostles in the Gospel, are also to eat of the Gospel. He gives clear illustrations in verses 7-12, that workers of the gospel should eat of the field that they work and plow in.

Group Activity 1

13] Do ye not know that they which minister about holy things live of the things of the temple? and they which wait at the altar are partakers with the altar? [14] Even so hath the Lord ordained that they which preach the gospel should live of the gospel.

7. **The book of I Corth 16:1-2, How to Collect for The Church and The Saints:**

   1 Cor. 16:1-2 *Now concerning the collection for the saints, as I have given order to the churches of Galatia, even so do ye. [2] Upon the first day of the week let every one of you lay by him in store, as God hath prospered him, that there be no gatherings when I come.*

The first day of the week is generally known as Sunday. Here we can see that the collections for the church and the saints was of a divine order. Paul was appointed by God as an Apostle.

Paul goes on to say that even though the offerings are approved of God, yet it is your servant attitude to all that allows you to gain more, when you give willingly.

   1 Cor. 9:19 *For though I be free from all men, yet have I made myself servant unto all, that I might gain the more.*

8. **Why it is important to give: Read I Kings 17:7-17,** about the widows morsel of bread and water and II Kings 4:1-7, widow's oil and vessels to gain a deeper understanding of how faith works in the believers who give their last to bless someone else and in return gain an everlasting blessing.

   1 Kings 17:7-16 *[7] And it came to pass after a while, that the brook dried up, because there had been no rain in the land. [8] And the word of the Lord came unto him, saying, [9] Arise, get thee to Zarephath, which belongeth to Zidon, and dwell there: behold, I have commanded a widow woman there to sustain thee.*

   [10] So he arose and went to Zarephath. And when he came to the gate of the city, behold, the widow woman was there gathering of sticks: and he called to her, and said, Fetch me, I pray thee, a little water in a vessel, that I may drink. [11] And as she was going to fetch it, he called to her, and said, Bring me, I pray thee, a morsel of bread in thine hand.

GOD'S PLAN FOR AN ABUNDANT LIFE: Stewardship, Tithing & Discipleship

Group Activity 1

Read verse 10 carefully and identify what you think the widow was thinking about when Elijah appears to her.

- What was the widow preparing to fix? _____

_____

- Why did he want the morsel of bread in her hand? _____

_____

[12] And she said, As the Lord thy God liveth, I have not a cake, but an handful of meal in a barrel, and a little oil in a cruse: and, behold, I am gathering two sticks, that I may go in and dress it for me and my son, that we may eat it, and die. [13] And Elijah said unto her, Fear not; go and do as thou hast said: but make me thereof a little cake first, and bring it unto me, and after make for thee and for thy son. [14] For thus saith the Lord God of Israel, The barrel of meal shall not waste, neither shall the cruse of oil fail, until the day that the Lord sendeth rain upon the earth. [15] And she went and did according to the saying of Elijah: and she, and he, and her house, did eat many days. [16] And the barrel of meal wasted not, neither did the cruse of oil fail, according to the word of the Lord, which he spake by Elijah.

Did the widow do as Elijah asked? _____ What was the result of her faithfulness in giving?

Explain: _____

_____

_____

9. **Read II Kings 4:1-7, which tells of another story about giving. Write examples that will help ministries and the congregation remember the importance of giving their tithes and offerings.**

2 Kings 4:1-7 Now there cried a certain woman of the wives of the sons of the

Group Activity 1

prophets unto Elisha, saying, Thy servant my husband is dead; and thou knowest that thy servant did fear the Lord: and the creditor is come to take unto him my two sons to be bondmen. [2] And Elisha said unto her, What shall I do for thee? tell me, what hast thou in the house? And she said, Thine handmaid hath not any thing in the house, save a pot of oil. [3] Then he said, Go, borrow thee vessels abroad of all thy neighbours, even empty vessels; borrow not a few. [4] And when thou art come in, thou shalt shut the door upon thee and upon thy sons, and shalt pour out into all those vessels, and thou shalt set aside that which is full. [5] So she went from him, and shut the door upon her and upon her sons, who brought the vessels to her; and she poured out. [6] And it came to pass, when the vessels were full, that she said unto her son, Bring me yet a vessel. And he said unto her, There is not a vessel more. And the oil stayed. [7] Then she came and told the man of God. And he said, Go, sell the oil, and pay thy debt, and live thou and thy children of the rest.

_____
_____
_____
_____
_____
_____
_____
_____
_____
_____
_____
_____

GOD'S PLAN FOR AN ABUNDANT LIFE: Stewardship, Tithing & Discipleship

Group Activity 2
The Three T's:

The Three T's are important principles that we must grow to live by. Therefore, identify and discuss within your group what key points can be shared to help us use our: Time, Talents and Treasures in spreading the Gospel and how your life can be a blessing for others.

1. **Time = Service To God**

    a. God Created Time for Prayer, Praise, and Worship

    b. Study the Word of God

    c. Live life to Glorify God

2. **Talents = Gifts: Jesus the Greatest Gift to Carry Out His Work**

    a. God gave gifts to help equip man to spread the Gospel

    b. Edify, Exhort, and bring Comfort to the Body of Christ

3. **Treasures = The Holy Spirit Releases The Anointing, Blessings, Riches, Health, Wisdom, Knowledge, Understanding, and Money**

    a. Pay Tithes and give your offerings

    b. Support the Pastor/Minister

    c. Ministry can go forward

    d. Spread the Gospel and meet the needs of God's people

GOD'S PLAN FOR AN ABUNDANT LIFE: Stewardship, Tithing & Discipleship

Group Activity 2

BIBLE TRUTHS

God Is The Provider

James 1:17 *Every good gift and every perfect gift is from above, and cometh down from the Father of lights, with whom is no variableness, neither shadow of turning. KJV.*

Gen 22:7-8, 14 *7. And Isaac spake unto Abraham his father, and said, My father: and he said, Here am I, my son. And he said, Behold the fire and the wood: but where is the lamb for a burnt offering? 8. And Abraham said, My son, God will provide himself a lamb for a burnt offering: so they went both of them together. 14. And Abraham called the name of that place Jehovah-jireh: as it is said to this day, In the mount of the LORD it shall be seen. KJV*

Exercise: See the RU Factors, next page.

Give an example about what Abraham must have felt, and relate it to paying your tithes and giving your offerings.

_____
_____
_____

MY NOTES: _____
_____
_____
_____
_____
_____

GOD'S PLAN FOR AN ABUNDANT LIFE: Stewardship, Tithing & Discipleship

RU Factors: *The Are You (RU) Factors:*

1. RU you a person who asks yourself and God Why Tithe? Why Give? Why Sow?
2. RU you in debt or financial bondage?
3. RU an owner of several credit cards?
4. RU spending more and saving less?
5. RU giving more and gaining less?
6. RU one paycheck away from being broke?
7. RU robbing Peter to pay Paul?
8. RU feeling frustrated because you just do not have enough money or peace of mind?
9. RU a tither?
10. RU spending quality time in your prayer life?
11. RU using your God given gifts?
12. RU using your gifts to please God?
13. RU laying up your treasures on earth?
14. RU volunteering time to a ministry?
15. RU volunteering to help people in need?
16. RU you leading others to Christ Jesus by your lifestyle and work?
17. RU robbing God?
18. RU tithing and giving an offering according to God's Plan?
19. RU willing to live and tithe according to God's plan of stewardship?
20. RU part of God's Discipleship?

GOD'S PLAN FOR AN ABUNDANT LIFE: Stewardship, Tithing & Discipleship

Your Tithes and Offerings: A Covenant Commitment Between You and God

Transformed by the Renewing of Your Mind

Romans 12:1-2 *I beseech you therefore, brethren, by the mercies of God, that ye present your bodies a living sacrifice, holy, acceptable unto God, which is your reasonable service. [2] And be not conformed to this world: but be ye transformed by the renewing of your mind, that ye may prove what is that good, and acceptable, and perfect, will of God.*

This is God's Way of Life and The Keys to Your Inheritance: Phil. 4:6-7)

- Seeking God With A Repentant Heart Mt. 7:7

- Prayer and Fasting (Supplications and Thanksgiving)

- Praise and Worship

- Studying His Word 2 Tim. 2:15

- Watching and listening for the Word of God in your life

- The Holy Spirit is waiting for you to step out of yourself and into an abundant life of the fruit of the spirit

- **Galatians 5:22-23** the fruit of the Spirit is:
    - love
    - joy
    - peace
    - longsuffering
    - gentleness
    - goodness
    - faith
    - meekness
    - temperance: against such there is no law

GOD'S PLAN FOR AN ABUNDANT LIFE: Stewardship, Tithing & Discipleship

Group Activity 2

God's Abundant Glory: Promised To Those Who Keep His Word:

Deut 28:1-14 *And it shall come to pass, if thou shalt hearken diligently unto the voice of the Lord thy God, to observe and to do all his commandments which I command thee this day, that the Lord thy God will set thee on high above all nations of the earth: [2] And all these blessings shall come on thee, and overtake thee, if thou shalt hearken unto the voice of the Lord thy God. [3] Blessed shalt thou be in the city, and blessed shalt thou be in the field. [4] Blessed shall be the fruit of thy body, and the fruit of thy ground, and the fruit of thy cattle, the increase of thy kine, and the flocks of thy sheep. [5] Blessed shall be thy basket and thy store. [6] Blessed shalt thou be when thou comest in, and blessed shalt thou be when thou goest out. [7] The Lord shall cause thine enemies that rise up against thee to be smitten before thy face: the blessing upon thee in thy storehouses, and in all that thou settest thine hand unto; and he shall bless thee in the land which the Lord thy God giveth thee. [9] The Lord shall establish thee an holy people unto himself, as he hath sworn unto thee, if thou shalt keep the commandments of the Lord thy God, and walk in his ways. [10] And all people of the earth shall see that thou art called by the name of the Lord; and they shall be afraid of thee. [11] And the Lord shall make thee plenteous in goods, in the fruit of thy body, and in the fruit of thy cattle, and in the fruit of thy ground, in the land which the Lord sware unto thy fathers to give thee. [12] The Lord shall open unto thee his good treasure, the heaven to give the rain unto thy land in his season, and to bless all the work of thine hand: and thou shalt lend unto many nations, and thou shalt not borrow. [13] And the Lord shall make thee the head, and not the tail; and thou shalt be above only, and thou shalt not be beneath; if that thou hearken unto the commandments of the Lord thy God, which I command thee this day, to observe and to do them:*
[14] And thou shalt not go aside from any of the words which I command thee this day, to the right hand, or to the left, to go after other gods to serve them.

Group Activity 2

Key Factors That Help Develop A Life of Giving To God Your Tithes & Offering:

Seek The Kingdom of God:
    Matthew 6:33 *Seek Ye First The Kingdom of God and His Righteousness and All These Things Will Be Added Unto You*

Put On The Fruit of The Spirit:
    Galatians 5:22-23 *But the fruit of the Spirit is love, joy, peace, longsuffering, gentleness, goodness, faith, [23] Meekness, temperance: against such there is no law.*

Understand the Key Factors of:

1. **Wisdom:**

    Proverbs 3:1-20 *(Proverbs 3:9-10) Honour the Lord with thy substance, and with the firstfruits of all thine increase: [10] So shall thy barns be filled with plenty, and thy presses shall burst out with new wine.*

    Exodus 31:3 *And I have filled him with the spirit of God, in wisdom, and in understanding, and inknowledge, and in all manner of workmanship,*

    Proverbs 9:10 *The fear of the Lord is the beginning of wisdom: and the knowledge of the holy is understanding.*

2. **Knowledge:**

    II Chron. 1:11-12 *And God said to Solomon, Because this was in thine heart, and thou hast not asked riches, wealth, or honour, nor the life of thine enemies, neither yet hast asked long life; but hast asked wisdom and knowledge for thyself, that thou mayest judge my people, over whom I have made thee king: [12] Wisdom and knowledge is granted unto thee; and I will give thee riches, and wealth, and honour, such as none of the kings have had that have been before thee, neither shall there any after thee have the like.*

    Proverbs 1:7 *The fear of the Lord is the beginning of knowledge: but fools despise wisdom and instruction.*

GOD'S PLAN FOR AN ABUNDANT LIFE: Stewardship, Tithing & Discipleship

Group Activity 2

Proverbs 2:1-4 *My son, if thou wilt receive my words, and hide my commandments with thee; [2] So that thou incline thine ear unto wisdom, and apply thine heart to understanding; [3] Yea, if thou criest after knowledge, and liftest up thy voice for understanding; [4] If thou seekest her as silver, and searchest for her as for hidden treasures;*

For the Lord giveth wisdom: out of his mouth cometh knowledge and understanding.

Proverbs 2:5-6 *Then shalt thou understand the fear of the Lord, and find the knowledge of God. For the Lord giveth wisdom: out of his mouth cometh knowledge and understanding.*

Proverbs 4:7 *Wisdom is the principal thing; therefore get wisdom: and with all thy getting get understanding.*

3. Understanding: In All Thy Getting Get Understanding

Job 32:8 *But there is a spirit in man: and the inspiration of the Almighty giveth them understanding.*

Proverbs 1:5 *A wise man will hear, and will increase learning; and a man of understanding shall attain unto wise counsels:*

Proverbs 2:11 *Discretion shall preserve thee, understanding shall keep thee:*

Proverbs 4:5-6 *Get wisdom, get understanding: forget it not; neither decline from the words of my mouth. Forsake her not, and she shall preserve thee: love her, and she shall keep thee.*

Proverbs 4:7 *Wisdom is the principal thing; therefore get wisdom: and with all thy getting get understanding.*

78

Group Activity 3

I. Discipleship & Stewardship are God's Plan for a Spirit-filled Life:

A. **Spiritual Growth is Financial Freedom** (Luke.16:10-13)

Luke 16:10-13 *He that is faithful in that which is least is faithful also in much: and he that is unjust in the least is unjust also in much. [11] If therefore ye have not been faithful in the unrighteous mammon, who will commit to your trust the true riches? [12] And if ye have not been faithful in that which is another man's, who shall give you that which is your own? [13] No servant can serve two masters: for either he will hate the one, and love the other; or else he will hold to the one, and despise the other. Ye cannot serve God and mammon.*

I Timothy 5:17-18 *Let the elders that rule well be counted worthy of double honour, especially they who labour in the word and doctrine. 18For the scripture saith, Thou shalt not muzzle the ox that treadeth out the corn. II Timothy 5:17-18*

B. **What Debt Does:**
1. A Bond for Materialism vs. for Christ Jesus

2 Tim. 2:4 *No one serving as a soldier gets involved in civilian affairs—he wants to please his commanding officer.*

Galatians 4:9 *But now, after that ye have known God, or rather are known of God, how turn ye again to the weak and beggarly elements, whereunto ye desire again to be in bondage?*

Proverb 22: 7 *The rich ruleth over the poor, and the borrower is servant to the lender. (See Deut.15:6, (1-11)*

2. **Weakens Your Relationships With God (Slaves for Money). (Money as an Idol, see I Corth.10:14)**

Matthew 6:24 *"No one can serve two masters. Either he will hate the one and love the other, or he will be devoted to the one and despise the other. You cannot serve both God and Money.*

Group Activity 3

3. Hinders Doing God's Will for Your Future
Matthew 6:34 *Take therefore no thought for the morrow: for the morrow shall take thought for the things of itself. Sufficient unto the day is the evil thereof. (Deut 28:15)*

4. Creates Stress, Worry, Fear and Doubt
Matthew 6:19-21 *Lay not up for yourselves treasures upon earth, where moth and rust doth corrupt, and where thieves break through and steal: [20] But lay up for yourselves treasures in heaven, where neither moth nor rust doth corrupt, and where thieves do not break through nor steal: [21]For where your treasure is, there will your heart be also.*

Matthew 6:25 *"Therefore I tell you, do not worry about your life what you will eat or drink; or about your body, what you will wear. Is not life more important than food, and the body more important than clothes?"*

Matthew 6:28 *"And why do you worry about clothes? See how the lilies of the field grow. They do not labor or spin."*

C. Results of Not Following God's Plan:

1. Rusted Treasures
Matthew 6:19 *Lay not up for yourselves treasures upon earth, where moth and rust doth corrupt, and where thieves break through and steal:*

James 5:3 *Your gold and silver is cankered; and the rust of them shall be a witness against you, and shall eat your flesh as it were fire. Ye have heaped treasure together for the last days.*

2. Dependent upon borrowing
Deut. 15:6 *For the Lord your God will bless you as he has promised, and you will lend to many nations but will borrow from none. You will rule over many nations but none will rule over you.*

> *But lay up for yourselves treasures in heaven, where neither moth nor rust doth corrupt, and where thieves do not break through nor steal...*

Group Activity 3

3. **Trusting In God's Word**
   2 Samuel 22:3 *The God of my rock; in him will I trust: he is my shield, and the horn of my salvation, my high tower, and my refuge, my saviour; thou savest me from violence.*

4. **Will Miss the Glory and the Joy of God's Promise**
   Jude 1:23-25 *And others save with fear, pulling them out of the fire; hating even the garment spotted by the flesh. [24] Now unto him that is able to keep you from falling, and to present you faultless before the presence of his glory with exceeding joy, [25] To the only wise God our Saviour, be glory and majesty, dominion and power, both now and ever. Amen.*

   Proverbs 25:2 *It is the glory of God to conceal a thing: but the honour of kings is to search out a matter.*

   Romans 11:33 *God's riches, wisdom, and knowledge are so deep that it is impossible to explain his decisions or to understand his ways.* GW

   Romans 11:33 *O the depth of the riches both of the wisdom and knowledge of God! how unsearchable are his judgments, and his ways past finding out!*

D. **Quick Steps Into Poverty and The Spirit of Lack: God's Warning About Desiring Riches and Trusting Riches of the Flesh**

   1. **Selfishness**
      Proverbs 11:24 *One man gives freely, yet gains even more; another withholds unduly, but comes to poverty.*

      2 Cor. 9:6-7 *But this I say, He which soweth sparingly shall reap also sparingly; and he which soweth bountifully shall reap also bountifully, (7) Every man according as he purposeth in his heart, so let him give; not grudgingly, or of necessity: for God loveth a cheerful giver.*

   2. **Seeking Riches**
      Proverbs 23:4-5 *Labour not to be rich: cease from thine own wisdom. [5] Wilt thou set thine eyes upon that which is not? for riches certainly make themselves wings; they fly away as an eagle toward heaven.*

Group Activity 3

Proverbs 28:22 He that hasteth to be rich hath an evil eye, and considereth not that poverty shall come upon him.

Luke 6:24 But woe unto you that are rich! for ye have received your consolation.

Matthew 13:22 He also that received seed among the thorns is he that heareth the word; and the care of this world, and the deceitfulness of riches, choke the word, and he becometh unfruitful.

Matthew 13:23 But he that received seed into the good ground is he that heareth the word, and understandeth it; which also beareth fruit, and bringeth forth, some an hundredfold, some sixty, some thirty.

Luke 12:14-16 And he said unto him, Man, who made me a judge or a divider over you? [15] And he said unto them, Take heed, and beware of covetousness: for a man's life consisteth not in the abundance of the things which he possesseth. [16] And he spake a parable unto them, saying, The ground of a certain rich man brought forth plentifully:

For the love of money is the root of all evil: which while some coveted after, they have erred from the faith, and pierced themselves through with many sorrows.

1 Tim. 6:7-10 For we brought nothing into this world, and it is certain we can carry nothing out. [8] And having food and raiment let us be therewith content. [9] But they that will be rich fall into temptation and a snare, and into many foolish and hurtful lusts, which drown men in destruction and perdition. [10] For the love of money is the root of all evil: which while some coveted after, they have erred from the faith, and pierced themselves through with many sorrows. [11] But thou, O man of God, flee these things; and follow after righteousness, godliness, faith, love, patience, meekness.

1 Cor. 6:9 Know ye not that the unrighteous shall not inherit the kingdom of God? Be not deceived: neither fornicators, nor idolaters, nor adulterers, nor effeminate, nor abusers of themselves with mankind,

2 Tim. 2:22 Flee also youthful lusts: but follow righteousness, faith, charity, peace, with them that call on the Lord out of a pure heart.

Group Activity 3

1 Tim. 6:17-18 *Charge them that are rich in this world, that they be not highminded, nor trust in uncertain riches, but in the living God, who giveth us richly all things to enjoy; [18] That they do good, that they be rich in good works, ready to distribute, willing to communicate;*

3. A Sluggards Mentality

Proverbs 13:4 *The sluggard craves and gets nothing, but the desires of the diligent are fully satisfied.*

Proverbs 20:13 *Do not love sleep or you will grow poor; stay awake and you will have food to spare.*

4. Driven to be Rich and Full of Vanity

Proverbs 28:19-20 *He that tilleth his land shall have plenty of bread: but he that followeth after vain persons shall have poverty enough. [20] A faithful man shall abound with blessings: but he that maketh haste to be rich shall not be innocent.*

Proverbs 12:11 *He that tilleth his land shall be satisfied with bread: but he that followeth vain persons is void of understanding.*

Proverbs 11:28 *He that trusteth in his riches shall fall: but the righteous shall flourish as a branch.*

Proverbs 22:16 *He that oppresseth the poor to increase his riches, and he that giveth to the rich, shall surely come to want.*

Jeremiah 9:23 *Thus saith the Lord, Let not the wise man glory in his wisdom, neither let the mighty man glory in his might, let not the rich man glory in his riches:*

Romans 8:6 *for to be carnally minded is death; but to be spiritually minded is life and peace.*

Romans 8:13 *For if ye live after the flesh, ye shall die: but if ye through the Spirit do mortify the deeds of the body, ye shall live.*

Galatians 6:8 *For he that soweth to his flesh shall of the flesh reap corruption; but he that soweth to the Spirit shall of the Spirit reap life everlasting.*

Group Activity 3

E. When God Is In Control of Your Finances
1. God is the Owner

Deut. 10:14 *Behold, the heaven and the heaven of heavens is the Lord's thy God, the earth also, with all that therein is.*

Acts 17:24 *God that made the world and all things therein, seeing that he is Lord of heaven and earth, dwelleth not in temples made with hands;*

Psalm 50:10 *for every animal of the forest is mine, and the cattle on a thousand hills.*

2 Cor. 9:8-11 *And God is able to make all grace abound toward you; that ye, always having all sufficiency in all things, may abound to every good work: [9] (As it is written, He hath dispersed abroad; he hath given to the poor: his righteousness remaineth for ever. [10] Now he that ministereth seed to the sower both minister bread for your food, and multiply your seed sown, and increase the fruits of your righteousness;) [11] Being enriched in every thing to all bountifulness, which causeth through us thanksgiving to God.*

2. He Wants to Bless You

Deut 28: 1-6 *And all these blessings shall come on thee, and overtake thee, if thou shalt hearken unto the voice of the Lord Thy God. [3] Blessed shalt thou be in the city, a and blessed shalt thou be in the field. [4] Blessed shall be the fruit of thy body, and the fruit of thy ground, and the fruit of thy cattle, the increase of thy kine, and the flocks of thy sheep. [5] Blessed shall be thy basket and thy store. [6] Blessed shalt thou be when thou comest In and blessed shalt thou be when thou goest out.*

Exodus 23:24-25 *Thou shalt not bow down to their gods, nor serve them, nor do after their works: but thou shalt utterly overthrow them, and quite break down their images. [25] And ye shall serve the Lord your God, and he shall bless thy bread, and thy water; and I will take sickness away from the midst of thee.*

3. He Can Do Exceedingly: According To His Riches In Glory

Ephes. 3:18-21 *May be able to comprehend with all saints what is the breadth, and length, and depth, and height; [19] And to know the love of Christ, which passeth knowledge, that ye might be filled with all the fulness of God. [20] Now unto him that is able to do exceeding abundantly above all that we ask or think, according to the power that worketh in us, [21] Unto him be glory in the church by Christ Jesus throughout all ages, world without end. Amen.*

Group Activity 3

Philip. 4:13 *I can do all things through Christ which strengtheneth me.*

Ephes. 3:3 *How that by revelation he made known unto me the mystery; (as I wrote afore in few words,*

Ephes. 3:9 *And to make all men see what is the fellowship of the mystery, which from the beginning of the world hath been hid in God, who created all things by Jesus Christ:*

Col. 1:26 -29 *Whereof I am made a minister, according to the dispensation of God which is given to me for you, to fulfil the word of God; [26] Even the mystery which hath been hid from ages and from generations, but now is made manifest to his saints: [27] To whom God would make known what is the riches of the glory of this mystery among the Gentiles; which is Christ in you, the hope of glory: [28] Whom we preach, warning every man, and teaching every man in all wisdom; that we may present every man perfect in Christ Jesus: [29] Whereunto I also labour, striving according to his working, which worketh in me mightily.*

> *I can do all things through Christ which strengtheneth me.*

4. He Who Gives Good Gifts

Matthew 7:7-12 *Ask, and it shall be given you; seek, and ye shall find; knock, and it shall be opened unto you: [8] For every one that aasketh receiveth; and he that seeketh findeth; and to him that knocketh it shall be opened. [9] Or what man is there of you, whom if his son ask bread, will he give him a stone? [10] Or if he ask a fish, will he give him a serpent? [11] If ye then, being evil, know how to give good gifts unto your children, how much more shall your Father which is in heaven give good things to them that ask him? [12] Therefore all things whatsoever ye would that men should do to you, do ye even so to them: for this is the law and the prophets.*

Psalm 84:11 *For the Lord God is a sun and shield: the Lord will give grace and glory: no good thing will he withhold from them that walk uprightly.*

James 1:17 *Every good gift and every perfect gift is from above, and cometh down from the Father of lights, with whom is no variableness, neither shadow of turning.*

Group Activity 3

It Is Not What It Looks Like: Believe and Operate In Faith

5. **Mark 11:20-23** *And in the morning, as they passed by, they saw the fig tree dried up from the roots. [21] And Peter calling to remembrance saith unto him, Master, behold, the fig tree which thou cursedst is withered away. [22] And Jesus answering saith unto them, Have faith in God. [23] For verily I say unto you, That whosoever shall say unto this mountain, Be thou removed, and be thou cast into the sea; and shall not doubt in his heart, but shall believe that those things which he saith shall come to pass; he shall have whatsoever he saith.*

6. **The Power of Prayer: When You Pray Believing You Have Received Then by Faith You Shall Have The Desires of Your Heart.**

    Mark 11:24 *Therefore I say unto you, What things soever ye desire, when ye pray, believe that ye receive them, and ye shall have them.*

7. **Give and Forgive and Leave Your Offering At The Alter**

    Mark 11:25-26 *[25] And when ye stand praying, forgive, if ye have ought against any: that your Father also which is in heaven may forgive you your trespasses. [26] But if ye do not forgive, neither will your Father which is in heaven forgive your trespasses.*

    Matthew 5:23 *Therefore if thou bring thy gift to the altar, and there rememberest that thy brother hath ought against thee;*

    Romans 5:8 *Christ died for us while we were still sinners. This demonstrates God's love for us.*

F. **God Wants The Church United and On One Accord**
   1. Being of Like Mind   Phil. 2:2
   2. Diversities of Gifts   1 Cor. 12:4
   3. Unity of Faith   Eph. 4:13
   4. Gifts of the Church   Eph. 4:3-12
   5. One Spirit and One Body   I Corth. 14:4-13

Group Activity 3

G. Godly Principles:

1.	Ownership of God	(Deut 10:13-15)
2.	God knows the desires of your heart	(Ps. 37:1-7)
3.	God has a plan for you	(Jer.29:11)
4.	To receive wisdom, knowledge, and get understanding	(Prov. 2:10-11; 3:19-20; 4:5-9; Ps. 49:1-3; 51:1-6)
5.	Gives Revelations	II Corth 12:1-10
6.	Be a Faithful Steward	(Prov. 8:11-12; 9:1)
7.	Gives Testimonies	(Ps.25:13-14; Prov.10:22)
8.	Abundance and prosperity	(Ps. 37:11; Prov. 24:1-4)
9.	Eternal Salvation	(Rm. 1:16; !0:9-13)
10.	Protection, deliverance and healing	(Ps. 51:7-10; 110:10; Prov.1:7)

H. God's Blessing Released To The Children of God:

1. God will provide your every need
2. He is over your finances
3. Wisdom and Long Life
4. Provider for His Children
5. Prosperity
6. Wealth
7. Favor
8. Grace and Mercy
9. Redemption
10. Everlasting Life

II. Principles of Giving: According to Paul

1.	To support the Church	I Tim 5:17,18;
2.	It's right	I Corth. 9; v. 7, 8
3.	Old Testament Laws/examples	v. 9-11, 13
4.	New Testament	v. 12
5.	Jesus teaches	v. 14
6.	You are a Treasure in an Earthly Vessel,	II Corth. 4:7

GOD'S PLAN FOR AN ABUNDANT LIFE: Stewardship, Tithing & Discipleship

Group Activity 3

III. Why The Church Must Teach Stewardship, Tithing, & Discipleship

1. God's Word and His Way
2. Gives spiritual freedom
3. Biblically correct
4. Spreads the Gospel
5. Draws men to God and saves souls
6. Leads to Salvation and spiritual development
7. Releases the Gifts to the Church
8. Destroys debt and the spirit of lack
9. Eliminates the need for church fund raising
10. Supplies all the needs of the church
11. Provides for the needy
12. Supports the expansion of ministries
13. Increase and enhances intimate relationships with God
14. Blesses the congregation, families, and neighborhood
15. Requires self-denial
16. Provides for the Pastor and ministerial staff
17. Expands church development

GOD'S PLAN FOR AN ABUNDANT LIFE: Stewardship, Tithing & Discipleship

Why We Give...

I. Why Give to God?

A. **Because He is our Creator:**

Genesis 1:1 *In the beginning God created the heaven and the earth.*

Genesis 1:26-28 *[26] And God said, Let us make man in our image, after our likeness: and let them have dominion over the fish of the sea, and over the fowl of the air, and over the cattle, and over all the earth, and over every creeping thing that creepeth upon the earth. [27] So God created man in his own image, in the image of God created he him; male and female created he them. [28] And God blessed them, and God said unto them, Be fruitful, and multiply, and replenish the earth, and subdue it: and have dominion over the fish of the sea, and over the fowl of the air, and over every living thing that moveth upon the earth.*

> *Greater love hath no man than this, that a man lay down his life for his friends*

B. **He gave his Son's life as a ransom for you and me:**

1 John 4:10 *Herein is love, not that we loved God, but that he loved us, and sent his Son to be the propitiation for our sins.*

John 15:13 *Greater love hath no man than this, that a man lay down his life for his friends.*

Matthew 20:28 *Even as the Son of man came not to be ministered unto, but to minister, and to give his life a ransom for many.*

1 Cor. 6:19-20 *[19] What? know ye not that your body is the temple of the Holy Ghost which is in you, which ye have of God, and ye are not your own? [20] For ye are bought with a price: therefore glorify God in your body, and in your spirit, which are God's.*

C. **It Is Your Reasonable Service:**

1. **God's people belong to Him by creation:**

Psalm 100:3-4 *Know ye that the Lord he is God: it is he that hath made us, and not we ourselves; we are his people, and the sheep of his pasture. [4] Enter into his gates with thanksgiving, and into his courts with praise: be thankful unto him, and bless his name. [5] For the Lord is good; his mercy is everlasting; and his truth endureth to all generations.*

Rev. 4:11 *Thou art worthy, O Lord, to receive glory and honor and power: for thou hast created all things, and for thy pleasure they are and were created.*

GOD'S PLAN FOR AN ABUNDANT LIFE: Stewardship, Tithing & Discipleship

Why We Give...

2. God is a Giver of All Good Things:

Deut. 8:18 But thou shalt remember the Lord thy God: **for it is he that giveth thee power to get wealth,** that he may establish his covenant which he sware unto thy fathers, as it is this day.

1 Chron. 29:14 But who am I, and what is my people, that we should be able to offer so willingly after this sort? for all things come of thee, and of thine own have we given thee.

1 Tim. 6:17-18 Charge them that are rich in this world, that they be not high-minded, nor trust in uncertain riches, **but in the living God, who giveth us richly all things to enjoy; [18] That they do good, that they be rich in good works, ready to distribute, willing to communicate;**

Acts 17:23-25: For as I passed by, and beheld your devotions, I found an altar with this inscription, TO THE UNKNOWN GOD. Whom therefore ye ignorantly worship, him declare I unto you. **[24] God that made the world and all things therein, seeing that he is Lord of heaven and earth, dwelleth not in temples made with hands;** [25] Neither is worshipped with men's hands, as though he needed any thing, seeing he giveth to all life, and breath, and all things;

Freely Give

2 Cor. 8:3 I assure you that by their own free will they have given all they could, even more than they could afford.

2 Cor. 8:3 For I testify that according to their ability, and beyond their ability they gave of their own accord, NASB

There are several differences between a Fund-Raising Campaign and A Stewardship Journey of Giving Back to God What He Created You To Manage:

As you have learned from previous teaching, Stewardship is the Fundamental Principals of Managing what God has created, including resources and countless blessings He stored up for you. You were created to manage God's Earthly Kingdom. You are God's greatest creation set over the perfected Garden of Eden, where you were given dominion to be: Fruitful, Multiply, Replenish, and to Subdue the Land.

Why We Give...

Pastors are called, anointed, ordained, and empowered by God to spread the Gospel. Your Pastor was placed over your life to bring you into a new relationship with God via his son Jesus Christ, see:

> **Jeremiah 3:15,** *And I will give you pastors according to mine heart, which shall feed you with knowledge and understanding.*

His responsibility includes feeding the sheep. As believers it is our responsibly to serve and to provide for the Pastor's wellbeing.

I. First, let me explain the difference between:

A. A Fundraiser

1. Is not in the Word of God
2. Is not a First Fruit Offering
3. Nullifies giving Tithes and Offerings with a Willing Heart
4. Blemishes your Offerings

B. About Fundraisers:

1. The funding, building of ministries, and the physical church building should not be done by fundraisers.

2. Fundraisers are ways to raise money based on collecting money from other people based on product(s) sold, work performed or just collecting donations.

3. This type of giving is blemished offerings. The intent is to give what is not yours and it cost you nothing. II Sam. 24:24

4. **Examples of fundraising are:**
    i. Selling products and services such as: candy sales, car washes, dinners, tickets for annual Church events, plays, musicals, operas, gospel concerts, fashion shows, promoting business ventures, helping to promote investment or insurance plans.

Why We Give...

  ii. It is promoting someone's entrepreneurship and they give the pastor something special for helping their cause, such as: Vitamins, books, insurance, clothes, candy, Christmas and holiday cards, pens & pencil sets, audio tapes and videos, just to name a few.

  iii. It requires selling and collecting but it is not a biblical principal.

  iv. It does not take the place of giving of your tithes and offerings.

C. A Fundraiser Is Not Biblical:
1. Money cannot raise you up

2. Only Christ Jesus can raise you from the dead

3. Fundraisers can not wash away your sins nor heal a Broken Heart, but Jesus will.

4. He hung His head and died on Calvary, giving up his life. He is now seated on the right hand of the Almighty God.

5. He died and arose to deliver us from hell and eternal damnation into the marvelous light.

6. By His Grace we receive the promise of salvation for the Glory of God.

II. God Wants Your Best Sacrificial Offering:

  A. It is the Truth in the Word of God

  B. He gives the Command to give Sacrificial Offerings

  C. It is your duty and responsibility to pay your Pastor's salary

  D. It is your responsibility to also pay for ministers and ministries

  E. It requires a Deeper Level of Sacrifice and Commitment

GOD'S PLAN FOR AN ABUNDANT LIFE: Stewardship, Tithing & Discipleship

Why We Give...

III. Giving Your Tithes and Offering:

   A. Honor God

   B. Is A Commandment of God

   C. Is A Tenth of Your Annual Incomes, With Spirit Filled Offerings

   D. Teaches Spiritual Discipline and Obedience To God's Word

   E. Bring Your Tithes To The Storehouse

   F. Giving A Sacrificial Offering

   G. Releases Blessings of God's Promise to Abraham's Seed

   H. Helps You To Trust God

Read in the Old Testament Mal. 3: 8-12 for a better understanding of "…will a man rob God?" Also read in the book of Leviticus 27:30 what God says about the tithe.

Leviticus 27:30 *And all the tithe of the land, whether of the seed of the land, or of the fruit of the tree, is the Lord's: it is holy unto the Lord.*

- Giving the tenth of what you own and your offering is what you give to worship God. Thanking God, for who he is, not because he gave you something or did something for you.

- Can you give an offering when times are difficult? The answer is, yes.

- You should always take time to worship God and bless him with your best offering.

- Do not stop at just saying you love and respect God. You need to Honor Him with your Tithes, Offerings, and Sacrificial Offering.

- We show respect when we treat people with love and kindness, or speak with a kind word. However, to Honor someone you need to value the person.

GOD'S PLAN FOR AN ABUNDANT LIFE: Stewardship, Tithing & Discipleship

Why We Give...

> The word **Honor** in Greek is pronounced **ti-me (tee-may')** and it means; a value added, as an example; it is money paid, or presenting valuables; it is to esteem, reverence (especially to the highest degree), or the dignity itself: honor, precious, or price.

In the Greek translation listed below are the meanings given for honor:

You can say you respect a person but never go out of the way to really give them much, or you offer very little or nothing.

Honor adds value to a deeper relationship. You not only follow the teaching of this individual but **you have established a fellowship with the person.** You have grown to trust, believing in the individual and knowing they have a trusting relationship in Faith. These believers have a higher level of integrity and honesty.

A preacher recently said that if you want a fellowship and citizenship with Jesus there first must be follow-ship. This requires humbling yourself and submitting to the ways of God.

Knowing that God is Worthy of Praise and Worship for what He has done for us; please explain what the following questions mean to you.

How do we Worship Him and what do we give to Honor and Value His Love for us?

_____
_____
_____
_____

How You Worship Jesus Is Reflected By How Worthy Jesus Is To You? Explain.

_____
_____
_____
_____

GOD'S PLAN FOR AN ABUNDANT LIFE: Stewardship, Tithing & Discipleship

Why We Give...

Theme: Sowing & Reaping—Your Abundant Harvest
Tilling The Land (Stewards of God's Garden)

The following is a sermon given to congregates, on the importance of understanding the Stewards' responsibility of tilling and sowing for Christ. Read and enjoy and by all means if you are challenged to become a tither, a servant of the Lord then we Praise God for the Word has fallen on Good Ground.

> **Genesis 1:11-13** *And God said, Let the earth bring forth grass, the herb yielding seed, and the fruit tree yielding fruit after his kind, whose seed is in itself, upon the earth: and it was so. [12] And the earth brought forth grass, and herb yielding seed after his kind, and the tree yielding fruit, whose seed was in itself, after his kind: and God saw that it was good. [13] And the evening and the morning were the third day.*

> **2 Cor. 9:6-7** *But this I say, He which soweth sparingly shall reap also sparingly; and he which soweth bountifully shall reap also bountifully. [7] Every man according as he purposeth in his heart, so let him give; not grudgingly, or of necessity: for God loveth a cheerful giver.*

PRAISE GOD: For He is Worthy of All Praise and Honor:

Foundational Principles on Sowing and Reaping Your Abundant Harvest:

Our Topic:	Tilling the Land (Stewards of God's Garden)
The Application:	Your Willing Obedience To God: Full-Fills God's Abrahamic Covenant:
Life Application Example:	"Giving Back To God With A Willing Heart"

GOD'S PLAN FOR AN ABUNDANT LIFE: Stewardship, Tithing & Discipleship

Why We Give...

Key Elements:

I. Accept, Believe, and Trust that God is the Creator and the Owner of Everything you have or will have. You Belong to God.

Expect a Miracle

I Cor. 3:6 *I have planted, Apollos watered; but God gave the increase.*

Psalm 24:1 *The earth is the Lord's, and the fulness thereof; the world, and they that dwell therein.*

II. Sow Your Seeds in Faith

Hebrews 11:1 *Now faith is the substance of things hoped for, the evidence of things not seen.*

III. Seek ye first the Kingdom of God and His Righteousness and all these things shall be added unto you Mt 6:33.

Mark 10:28-31 *Then Peter began to say unto him, Lo, we have left all, and have followed thee. [29] And Jesus answered and said, Verily I say unto you, There is no man that hath left house, or brethren, or sisters, or father, or mother, or wife, or children, or lands, for my sake, and the gospel's, [30] But he shall receive an hundredfold now in this time, houses, and brethren, and sisters, and mothers, and children, and lands, with persecutions; and in the world to come eternal life. [31] But many that are first shall be last; and the last first.*

IV. All seeds must be planted with and in Faith (Spiritual and Physical/Natural)

Your Faith is a seed and it will grow when you trust God and become more obedient to God's Word: Trusting in your Faith Seed comes when you can not:

- See
- Know
- Understand
- Explain

GOD'S PLAN FOR AN ABUNDANT LIFE: Stewardship, Tithing & Discipleship

Why We Give...

The Victorious and abundant Harvest, Breakthroughs, Deliverance, Healings, Promotions, Favor, and other seen and unseen manifested blessings come from God, through His Grace and Mercy.

V. A seed can not grow if it is not sown/planted; believing that there is an expected Abundant outcome, according to God's Word.

- Four Types of Ground We Sow Seeds In (Matt. 13:19-23)
- What type of Seeds are you Sowing?
- Where are you Sowing your Seeds?
- Is your Seed Blessed or Cursed?

1. Seeds Planted/Sown by the Wayside

Matthew 13:19 *When any one heareth the word of the Kingdom, and understandeth it not, then cometh the wicked one, and catcheth away that which was sown in his heart. This is he which received seed by the way side.*

2. Stony Places/Ground

Matthew 13:20 *But he that received the seed into stony places, the same is he that heareth the word, and anon with joy receiveth it;*

Matthew 13:21 *Yet hath he not root in himself, but dureth for a while: for when tribulation or persecution ariseth because of the word, by and by he is offended.*

3. Mixed Ground:

Matthew 13:22 *He also that received seed among the thorns is he that heareth the word; and the care of this world, and the deceitfulness of riches, choke the word, and he becometh unfruitful.*

4. Good Ground:

Matthew 13:23 *But he that received seed into the good ground is he that heareth the word, & understandeth it; which also beareth fruit, and bringeth forth, some an hundredfold, some sixty, some thirty.*

GOD'S PLAN FOR AN ABUNDANT LIFE: Stewardship, Tithing & Discipleship

Why We Give...

Other Key Sowing & Harvesting Factors:

VI. The seed must be (sowed, scattered), planted plentifully

Isaiah 44:3 *For I will pour water upon him that is thirsty, and floods upon the dry ground: I will pour my spirit upon thy seed, and my blessing upon thine offspring:*

VII. The seed must be planted in good ground

Matthew 13:8 *But other fell into good ground, and brought forth fruit, some an hundredfold, some sixtyfold, some thirtyfold.*

VIII. The seed must die (germinate) before it grows John 12:23-26

John 12:23-26 *And Jesus answered them, saying, The hour is come, that the Son of man should be glorified. [24] Verily, verily, I say unto you, Except a corn of wheat fall into the ground and die, it abideth alone: but if it die, it bringeth forth much fruit. [25] He that loveth his life shall lose it; and he that hateth his life in this world shall keep it unto life eternal. [26] If any man serve me, let him follow me; and where I am, there shall also my servant be: if any man serve me, him will my Father honour.*

IX. Sow the seeds you want to harvest

Genesis 1:12 *And the earth brought forth grass, and herb yielding seed after his kind, and the tree yielding fruit, whose seed was in itself, after his kind: and God saw that it was good.*

X. Multiply what you sow by sowing to your harvest size and not from your harvest size

Genesis 26:12 *Then Isaac sowed in that land, and received in the same year an hundredfold: and the Lord blessed him.*

Why We Give...

XI. The seed must be nurtured (soil must be tilled)

Matthew 13:7 *And some fell among thorns; and the thorns sprung up, and choked them:*

XII. The seed must be harvested at the right time

Mark 4:26-27 *And he said, So is the kingdom of God, as if a man should cast seed into the ground; [27] And should sleep, and rise night and day, and the seed should spring and grow up, he knoweth not how.*

XIII. The seed must be sowed /replanted again and again

Proverbs 11:24 *There is that scattereth, and yet increaseth; and there is that withholdeth more than is meet, but it tendeth to poverty.*

XIV. Your Harvest Size is Dependent upon the amount Sowed; Sow into your harvest not from your harvest

2 Cor. 9:6 *But this I say, He which soweth sparingly shall reap also sparingly; and he which soweth bountifully shall reap also bountifully.*

Why We Give...

How Can The People Hear Without A Pastor?

Jeremiah 3:14-16 *"Return, O backsliding children," says the Lord; "for I am married to you. I will take you, one from a city and two from a family, and I will bring you to Zion. [15] And I will give you shepherds according to My heart, who will feed you with knowledge and understanding. [16] Then it shall come to pass, when you are multiplied and increased in the land in those days," says the Lord, "that they will say no more, 'The ark of the covenant of the Lord.' It shall not come to mind, nor shall they remember it, nor shall they visit it, nor shall it be made anymore. NKJV*

Romans 10:11-21 *For the Scripture says, "Whoever believes on Him will not be put to shame." [12] For there is no distinction between Jew and Greek, for the same Lord over all is rich to all who call upon Him. [13] For "whoever calls on the name of the Lord shall be saved." [14] How then shall they call on Him in whom they have not believed? And how shall they believe in Him of whom they have not heard? And how shall they hear without a preacher?*

[15] And how shall they preach unless they are sent? As it is written: "How beautiful are the feet of those who preach the gospel of peace, Who bring glad tidings of good things!" [16] But they have not all obeyed the gospel. For Isaiah says, "Lord, who has believed our report?" [17] So then faith comes by hearing, and hearing by the word of God.

Stewardship Journey

Sacrificial Offerings are biblically rooted in God's Word. It is linked to Abraham in the Old Testament where tithes and offerings were established as law prior to the book of Leviticus. The Book of Laws dates back to the beginning of giving God tithes and offering.

I. **Giving should be a desire in your heart**

    A. Love the Lord with all the heart, mind, and soul. (MT. 22:37; MK 12:30)

    B. Your Pastor and ministers will not pressure you

GOD'S PLAN FOR AN ABUNDANT LIFE: Stewardship, Tithing & Discipleship

Why We Give...

C. Never give to God if you feel pressured because God will not honor your offerings

D. God only loves a cheerful giver. It must be precious in his sight

E. Sacrificial giving can never be tied to personal gain, promotion or selling products; that is referred to as fundraising

F. Your giving should be motivated by what God does, God's will for you, and not by what you want God to do for you

G. Your love for God cannot have selfish motives

H. Establish a disciplined life of prayer and meditation

II. Your Personal Worship Service to God Must Include Giving:

A. Take time with God: Prayer, Fasting, and Praise & Worship

B. You must establish a designated place in your home to pray

C. Schedule a specific time to pray by yourself or with family

D. Take time out for daily Devotion
1. This includes scripture reading
2. Praise/Worship Songs and Time for Godly Meditation

E. Begin to Journal:
1. Document what you are praying for
2. What are you asking God for?
3. What did you hear in your spirit?
4. Record what you did all day
5. What did you think about all day
6. Write down dreams and visions

GOD'S PLAN FOR AN ABUNDANT LIFE: Stewardship, Tithing & Discipleship

Why We Give...

III. You Must Trust God, And The God In Your Pastor

A. Pastor and leaders who embark on this journey should be living examples with Christ Centered lives.

B. If you are in a church that does not believe in teaching Tithes & Offering, pray and ask God to touch the heart of your Pastor.

C. Never ever speak against the man or woman of God. Never be the author of confusion or strife. It would be better for you to attend another church.

D. Pastors' Visions are Christ Centered
1. Catch the God given Vision of the Pastor for Church.
2. Pastors are called by God and placed in our lives.
3. Pastors are the Shepard's of the church.
4. They spend time daily with God.
5. They know specifically (or should know), what God's desire is for their church, members, community, city and state.

IV. Reason Why People Want To Give:

A. You have experienced the Blessings of God
B. You want to help spread the Gospel
C. You support the ministry
D. You have faith in God; He provides your every need
E. God is a provider and will meet your every need

> **Matthew 6:26** *behold the fowls of the air: for they sow not, neither do they reap, nor gather into barns; yet your heavenly Father feedeth them. Are ye not much better than they?*

> **Psalm 54:4** *behold, God is mine helper: the Lord is with them that uphold my soul.*

F. You are obedient to the things of God

GOD'S PLAN FOR AN ABUNDANT LIFE: Stewardship, Tithing & Discipleship

Why We Give...

G. Your desire to give
   a. You should not have to be reminded to give
   b. You give because you have a willing desire to be pleasing in the site of God...i.e. Sweet smell in his nostril

> **Philip. 4:18** *But I have all, and abound: I am full, having received of Epaphroditus the things which were sent from you, an odor of a sweet smell, a sacrifice acceptable, well-pleasing to God.*

> **Ephes. 5:2** *And walk in love, as Christ also hath loved us, and hath given himself for us an offering and a sacrifice to God for a sweet smelling savor.*

   c. We can all reference Bible illustrations of giving:
   - The widows mite; the widow and the lanterns; the widow and the morsel (bread)

> **1 Kings 17:15-16** *And she went and did according to the saying of Elijah: and she, and he, and her house, did eat many days. 16 And the barrel of meal wasted not, neither did the cruse of oil fail; according to the word of the Lord, which he spake by Elijah.*

> **Deut. 16:17** *Every man shall give as he is able, according to the blessing of the Lord thy God which he hath given thee.*

Consider how much you spend on stuff, the things you desire to purchase. You, like so many others, often waste more than you use. That is a sign of being undisciplined about your spending versus saving:

- Things we value and spend money on:
  - Ticket sells
  - New car
- In the world it is customary to pay $60 - $100,000 for a keynote speaker
- theaters for entertainment
- fashion shows

We give hotels thousands of dollars and we turn to our churches and give God the leftovers. We complain about giving to God, but we shout when we get the blessings.

GOD'S PLAN FOR AN ABUNDANT LIFE: Stewardship, Tithing & Discipleship

Why We Give...

H. Giving With A Willing Heart:

Exodus 25:1-2 *1. And the LORD spake unto Moses, saying, 2. speak unto the children of Israel, that they bring me an offering: of every man that giveth it willingly with his heart ye shall take my offering.*

I Chronicles 29:1-26 *Give With A Willing Heart "Moreover, because I have set my affection to the house of my God, I David..." again demonstrates his willingness to give for the building of the temple. This is also done to ask god to Bless the appointment of Solomon, his son, as King. This he did do demonstrate his affection (love) for God as an outward expression for the church congregates (people) to see.*

> *...for all that is in the heaven and in the earth is thine; thine is the kingdom, O LORD, and thou art exalted as head above all.*

...have of mine own proper good, of gold and silver, which I have given to the house of my God, over and above all that I have prepared for the holy house, Even three thousand talents of gold, of the gold of Ophir, and seven ...thousand talents of refined silver, to overlay the walls of the houses withal: The gold for things of gold, and the silver for things of silver, and for all manner of work to be made by the hands of artificers. And who then is willing to consecrate his service this day unto the LORD? Then the chief of the fathers and princes of the tribes of Israel, and the captains of thousands and of hundreds, with the rulers of the king's work, offered willingly.

Then the people rejoiced, for that they offered willingly, because with perfect heart they offered willingly to the LORD: and David the king also rejoiced with great joy.

David Offers Prayer To God: Thanking God for the Spirit of Giving

In verses 10-17 David renders a prayer of thanksgiving to the Lord our God, David acknowledges that everything we have comes from the Lord.

Wherefore David blessed the LORD before all the congregation: and David said, Blessed be thou, LORD God of Israel our father, for ever and ever. Thine, O LORD, is the greatness, and the power, and the glory, and the victory, and the majesty: for all that is in the heaven and in the earth is thine; thine is the kingdom, O LORD, and thou art exalted as head above all.

GOD'S PLAN FOR AN ABUNDANT LIFE: Stewardship, Tithing & Discipleship

Why We Give...

Both riches and honour come of thee, and thou reignest over all; and in thine hand is power and might; and in thine hand it is to make great, and to give strength unto all. Now therefore, our God, we thank thee, and praise thy glorious name. But who am I, and what is my people, that we should be able to offer so willingly after this sort?

- **for all things come of thee, and of thine own have we given thee.**

    RU **R**eally Giving Your All To God?
    RU Storing Your Tithe in God's Storehouse?

For we are strangers before thee, and sojourners, as were all our fathers: our days on the earth are as a shadow, and there is none abiding. O LORD our God, all this store that we have prepared to build thee an house for thine holy name cometh of thine hand, and is all thine own.

I know also, my God, that thou triest the heart, and hast pleasure in uprightness. As for me, in the uprightness of mine heart I have willingly offered all these things: and now have I seen with joy thy people, which are present here, to offer willingly unto thee.

I. II Corinthians 9:6-11 The Size of Your Sowing & Reaping What You Sow:

2 Cor. 9:5-11 *Therefore I thought it necessary to exhort the brethren, that they would go before unto you, and make up beforehand your bounty, whereof ye had notice before, that the same might be ready, as a matter of bounty, and not as of covetousness. [6] But this I say, He which soweth sparingly shall reap also sparingly; and he which soweth bountifully shall reap also bountifully. [7] Every man according as he purposeth in his heart, so let him give; not grudgingly, or of necessity: for God loveth a cheerful giver. [8] And God is able to make all grace abound toward you; that ye, always having all sufficiency in all things, may abound to every good work: [9] (As it is written, He hath dispersed abroad; he hath given to the poor: his righteousness remaineth for ever. [10] Now he that ministereth seed to the sower both minister bread for your food, and multiply your seed sown, and increase the fruits of your righteousness;) [11] Being enriched in every thing to all bountifulness, which causeth through us thanksgiving to God. [12] For the administration of this service not only supplieth the want of the saints, but is abundant also by many thanksgivings unto God;*

> *Every man according as he purposeth in his heart, so let him give; not grudgingly, or of necessity: for God loveth a cheerful giver.*

GOD'S PLAN FOR AN ABUNDANT LIFE: Stewardship, Tithing & Discipleship

Why We Give...

Genesis 14:18-24   Abram Gives To Melchizedek King of Salem

And Melchizedek king of Salem brought forth bread and wine: and he was the priest of the most high God. [19] And he blessed him, and said, Blessed be Abram of the most high God, possessor of heaven and earth: [20] And blessed be the most high God, which hath delivered thine enemies into thy hand. And he gave him tithes of all. [21] And the king of Sodom said unto Abram, Give me the persons, and take the goods to thyself. [22] And Abram said to the king of Sodom, I have lift up mine hand unto the Lord, the most high God, the possessor of heaven and earth, [23] That I will not take from a thread even to a shoelatchet, and that I will not take any thing that is thine, lest thou shouldest say, I have made Abram rich: [24] Save only that which the young men have eaten, and the portion of the men which went with me, Aner, Eshcol, and Mamre; let them take their portion.

> *The light of the body is the eye: if therefore thine eye be single, thy whole body shall be full of light.*

Matthew 6:19-22   Where are You Laying Your Treasures?

Lay not up for yourselves treasures upon earth, where moth and rust doth corrupt, and where thieves break through and steal: [20] But lay up for yourselves treasures in heaven, where neither moth nor rust doth corrupt, and where thieves do not break through nor steal: [21] For where your treasure is, there will your heart be also. [22] The light of the body is the eye: if therefore thine eye be single, thy whole body shall be full of light.

Matthew 6:22-28

No man can serve two masters: for either he will hate the one, and love the other; or else he will hold to the one, and despise the other. Ye cannot serve God and mammon.

Matthew 6:25-33   RU Giving All To God : Give No Thought:

Give No Thought To Worry and Anxiety   (See. Luke 12:22; Phil 4:6)

Therefore I say unto you, Take no thought for your life, what ye shall eat, or

GOD'S PLAN FOR AN ABUNDANT LIFE: Stewardship, Tithing & Discipleship

Why We Give...

what ye shall drink; nor yet for your body, what ye shall put on. Is not the life more than meat, and the body than raiment? [26] Behold the fowls of the air: for they sow not, neither do they reap, nor gather into barns; yet your heavenly Father feedeth them. Are ye not much better than they? [27] Which of you by taking thought can add one cubit unto his stature? [28] And why take ye thought for raiment? Consider the lilies of the field, how they grow; they toil not, neither do they spin: [29] And yet I say unto you, That even Solomon in all his glory was not arrayed like one of these. [30] Wherefore, if God so clothe the grass of the field, which to day is, and to morrow is cast into the oven, shall he not much more clothe you, O ye of little faith? [31] Therefore take no thought, saying, What shall we eat? or, What shall we drink? or, Wherewithal shall we be clothed? [32] (For after all these things do the Gentiles seek:) for your heavenly Father knoweth that ye have need of all these things.

Philippians 4:6-7   Trusting in God

In nothing be anxious; but in everything by prayer and supplication with thanksgiving let your requests be made known unto God. And the peace of God, which passeth all understanding, shall guard your hearts and your thoughts in Christ Jesus.

Matthew 6:33-34 Seek Ye first the Kingdom of God

But seek ye first the kingdom of God, and his righteousness; and all these things shall be added unto you. Take therefore no thought for the morrow: for the morrow shall take thought for the things of itself. Sufficient unto the day is the evil thereof.

Matthew 7:7 Golden Rule

Ask, and it shall be given you; seek, and ye shall find; knock, and it shall be opened unto you: For every one that asketh receiveth; and he that seeketh findeth; and to him that knocketh it shall be opened.

Ps 2:7-9 God Gives Power and Authority: To Take Back What The Devil Stole From Me

I will declare the decree: the LORD hath said unto me, Thou art my Son; this day have I begotten thee. Ask of me, and I shall give thee the heathen for thine inheritance, and the uttermost parts of the earth for thy possession. Thou shalt break them with a rod of iron; thou shalt dash them in pieces like a potter's vessel.

GOD'S PLAN FOR AN ABUNDANT LIFE: Stewardship, Tithing & Discipleship

Why We Give...

John 15:12-17   Christian Power of Attorney:
This is my commandment, That ye love one another, as I have loved you. Greater love hath no man than this, that a man lay down his life for his friends. Ye are my friends, if ye do whatsoever I command you. Henceforth I call you not servants; for the servant knoweth not what his lord doeth: but I have called you friends; for all things that I have heard of my Father I have made known unto you. Ye have not chosen me, but I have chosen you, and ordained you, that ye should go and bring forth fruit, and that your fruit should remain: that whatsoever ye shall ask of the Father in my name, he may give it you. These things I command you, that ye love one another.

ll Corth 5:17   Giving to God Begins The Transformations of Our Lives
Therefore if any man be in Christ, he is a new creature: old things are passed away; behold, all things are become new. And all things are of God, who hath reconciled us to himself by Jesus Christ, and hath given to us the ministry of reconciliation;

Rm 12:1-2   Be Ye Transformed It Is The Will of God:
I beseech you therefore, brethren, by the mercies of God, that ye present your bodies a living sacrifice, holy, acceptable unto God, which is your reasonable service. And be not conformed to this world: but be ye transformed by the renewing of your mind, that ye may prove what is that good, and acceptable, and perfect, will of God.

Job 42:10-12 Prayer and Faith: Releases and Restores God's Blessing and Your Inheritance
And the LORD turned the captivity of Job, when he prayed for his friends: also the LORD gave Job twice as much as he had before. Then came there unto him all his brethren, and all his sisters, and all they that had been of his acquaintance before, and did eat bread with him in his house: and they bemoaned him, and comforted him over all the evil that the LORD had brought upon him: every man also gave him a piece of money, and every one an earring of gold. So the LORD blessed the latter end of Job more than his beginning: for he had fourteen thousand sheep, and six thousand camels, and a thousand yoke of oxen, and a thousand she asses.

Proverbs 10:22   Your Riches Come From God
The blessing of the LORD, it maketh rich, and he addeth no sorrow with it.

GOD'S PLAN FOR AN ABUNDANT LIFE: Stewardship, Tithing & Discipleship

Why We Give...

Proverbs 3:1-10   The Key to Long Life and Peace

My son, forget not my law; but let thine heart keep my commandments: For length of days, and long life, and peace, shall they add to thee. Let not mercy and truth forsake thee: bind them about thy neck; write them upon the table of thine heart: So shalt thou find favour and good understanding in the sight of God and man. Trust in the LORD with all thine heart; and lean not unto thine own understanding. In all thy ways acknowledge him, and he shall direct thy paths. Be not wise in thine own eyes: fear the LORD, and depart from evil. It shall be health to thy navel, and marrow to thy bones. Honour the LORD with thy substance, and with the first fruits of all thine increase: So shall thy barns be filled with plenty, and thy presses shall burst out with new wine.

> *Honour the LORD with thy substance, and with the first fruits of all thine increase: So shall thy barns be filled with plenty, and thy presses shall burst out with new wine*

Genesis 12:1-3 The Blessings of God To Those Who Are Obedient

Now the LORD had said unto Abram, Get thee out of thy country, and from thy kindred, and from thy father's house, unto a land that I will shew thee: And I will make of thee a great nation, and I will bless thee, and make thy name great; and thou shalt be a blessing: And I will bless them that bless thee, and curse him that curseth thee: and in thee shall all families of the earth be blessed.

Isaiah 45: 3 Abundant Principles

And I will give thee the treasures of darkness, and hidden riches of secret places, that thou mayest know that I, the LORD, which call thee by thy name, am the God of Israel.

Luke 12:15   Be Aware of Vain Glory and Forsaking The Word of God

And he said unto them, Take heed, and beware of covetousness: for a man's life consisteth not in the abundance of the things which he possesseth.

Jeremiah 11:3-5   Cursed for Failing to Obey God's Word

And say thou unto them, Thus saith the LORD God of Israel; Cursed be the man that obeyeth not the words of this covenant, Which I commanded your fathers in the day that I brought

Why We Give...

them forth out of the land of Egypt, from the iron furnace, saying, Obey my voice, and do them, according to all which I command you: so shall ye be my people, and I will be your God: That I may perform the oath which I have sworn unto your fathers, to give them a land flowing with milk and honey, as it is this day. Then answered I, and said, So be it, O LORD.

Isaiah 10:27   Burdens Removed
And it shall come to pass in that day, that his burden shall be taken away from off thy shoulder, and his yoke from off thy neck, and the yoke shall be destroyed because of the anointing.

The Bible indicates that one of the most basic human tasks was to "till it and keep it" (Gen. 2:15, NRSV), so that human beings are seen as having divinely-given abilities to be gardeners or farmers. The close relationship between people and soil is also indicated by the similarity between two Hebrew words for man (adam) and earth (adamah).

Read Genesis 2:15
The Lord God put the man in the Garden of Eden to take care of it and to look after it. 16 But the Lord told him, "You may eat fruit from any tree in the garden." Man's responsibility in the garden of Eden indicates that sowing seeds and tilling the land, was and remains the illustration that gives the principles of sowing/planting and reaping.

Agriculture was also important in New Testament times. Jesus made frequent reference to the land and its products in His teaching, indicating that He and His hearers were quite familiar with such matters.

1The King James Version, (Cambridge: Cambridge) 1769.

GOD'S PLAN FOR AN ABUNDANT LIFE: Stewardship, Tithing & Discipleship

Notes

GOD'S PLAN FOR AN ABUNDANT LIFE: Stewardship, Tithing & Discipleship

Seminar 3

Discipleship
A Foundation For Tithing & Stewardship

Participant's Workbook

Evangelist Anton L. Seals, Sr.
VASTT Ministry

GOD'S PLAN FOR AN ABUNDANT LIFE: Stewardship, Tithing & Discipleship

Outline Of Seminar 3
Discipleship: A Foundaiton For Tithing & Stewardship

Discipleship: A Foundation For Tithing & Stewardship	**112**
Outline of Seminar 3	113
Introduction	114-116
What Is Discipleship	117-121
Disciples Have A Paradigm Shift In Their Thinking	122-123
Group Exercise On Discipleship Principles	124
Treasure Chest of Knowledge John 17:1-26	125
Christian Discipleship & Leadership Characteristic	126

John 17:1	Disciples Lift Up The Name of Jesus	126
V2	Disciples Have Power and Authority	126
V3	Disciples Have New Life	127
V4	Disciples Finish The Work	127
V5	Disciples Know God As The Alpha & Omega	128
V6	Disciples Teach & Live According To God' Word	128
V7-26	(Go to Page 129)	129

Disciples Love The Lord & Their Neighbors	130
Disciples Are Made Not Born	132
Study and Know the Truth	132-133
Prerequisites For Becoming A Disciple	133-135

Discipleship Group Exercise 136
    A Briefing For The Case Study 136-137
    Your Group Challenge 138
    Your Mission 138-140

Discipleship Group Exercise 141
    Instructions   No Greater Joy Than Knowing The Truth 141
    No Greater Joy Than Knowing The Truth 141
Twelve Principles of Discipleship 142
A Life of Discipleship & Stewardship 100% Tithers 143

Copyright © 2002 VASTT Ministry & Publishing

GOD'S PLAN FOR AN ABUNDANT LIFE: Stewardship, Tithing & Discipleship

Introduction

Dear Brothers and Sisters:

Regardless of your present Christian relationship and walk with Jesus, as a baby suckling on milk or mature meat eaters of God's Word, you are challenged to mature to a new, higher level of excellence in Christ. ***Therefore, it is my prayer that this training on Discipleship and Leadership will bring you into a fellowship and intimate relationship with Christ.*** This is not a casual training exercise that you are embarking on. The scriptures in your manual were given through the conviction and consecration of the Holy Spirit. Praying, believing, and trusting the desire is that the time you spend together in this seminar/workshop will have an everlasting and altering impact on the destiny of your life. ***The projected outcome of this training workshop will manifest itself through your being transformed, and becoming a new creature in Christ Jesus. This is your paradigm shift from where you used to be, where you presently are and where God is taking you in your future destiny.*** There will be inward signs, and outward signs, and marvelous works that are manifested wherever you go and whatever you do for the Glory of God. The Glory of God is the outpouring and manifestation of your gifts. It is your anointing being used to edify the Body of Christ (Church) and lead others to salvation through Christ Jesus. People will see God's Work in you. Let the Light of God in you pierce the darkness of your life. Let his light shine from your home and community. You can do all things through Christ, you just need to believe and trust in the Word of God. Do not remain comfortable with your present position or relationship with Jesus. Become more than just a follower of Jesus. Learn to hear his calling, leading and feel His presence. Become a doer of His Word.

Are you willing to wash the feet of the Shepard over you, or those of your co-workers, or church members that you do not feel comfortable with?

> **John 13:5** *After that he poureth water into a bason, and began to wash the disciples' feet, and to wipe them with the towel wherewith he was girded.*

> **John 13:14** *If I then, your Lord and Master, have washed your feet; ye also ought to wash one another's feet. For where the least of my people are, there I am also, said the Lord. You can not love me (Jesus), who you have never seen, without first loving your fellow brothers, who you may or may not know but you see them.*

GOD'S PLAN FOR AN ABUNDANT LIFE: Stewardship, Tithing & Discipleship

Introduction

> **Matthew 25:40** *And the King shall answer and say unto them, Verily I say unto you, Inasmuch as ye have done it unto one of the least of these my brethren, ye have done it unto me.*

Christian Leadership Exemplifies your Discipleship. It is an outpouring of Giving to God: Your **Treasures, Time, and Talents.**

The close relationship between the words discipline and disciple is obvious. The Disciples of Christ were required to live a disciplined life. Discipline removes inconsistencies, improves skills, allowing your gifts to come forth. The Word of God in you releases the anointing of your gifts.

> A **Disciple** is a disciplined servant willing to surrender their life to follow Christ and the covenants of the Father, for the Glory of God.
>
> A **Disciple** is one who follows or believes in the teachings or theories of someone, as in Jesus Christ.

Disciple refers to a larger group of Jesus' followers, such as the women who stood at Jesus' cross, and discovered the empty tomb. A follower demonstrates a willingness to accept, live by, and/or study established beliefs such as doctrines or covenants. **As a follower of Jesus Christ you have accepted** Him as your Savior. Therefore, as a Christian, your walk and conversation must reflect characteristics associated with God's chosen people.

A Disciple could be classified as a student, learner, or pupil. In the Bible the word is used most often to refer to a follower of Jesus. The word is rarely used in the Old Testament. Isaiah used the term "disciples", referring to those who are taught or instructed (Is. 8:16).

The word disciple references the twelve Apostles of Jesus, for future references read: (Matt. 10:1; 11:1; 20:17; Luke 9:1).

> **Matthew 10:1** *And **when he had called unto** him his twelve disciples, he gave them power against unclean spirits, to cast them out, and to heal all manner of sickness and all manner of disease.*

> **Matthew 20:17** *And Jesus going up to Jerusalem took the twelve disciples apart in the way, and said unto them,*

Introduction

Luke 9:1 *Then he called his twelve disciples together, and gave them power and authority over all devils, and to cure diseases.*

If you trust in what The Word of God Teaches about Discipleship, you will understand that your work is a ministry (service/servant) for Christ. Your willingness to serve in your church and community, beyond the gates, is an outward demonstration of your spiritual maturity as an obedient and disciplined follower of Christ Jesus. Obedient followers of Christ are called Disciples. Fruitful Disciples live disciplined lives that lead others to Christ. Leading, involves the ability to influence others to seek, follow, and accept Christ as their Lord and Savior.

Discipleship is one of the obligations, you have as believers, to our Lord and Savoir Jesus Christ. Jesus shows us how to live our lives. Jesus gives a living example of Discipleship. In the Gospel of St. John 17: 1-26. Jesus prays for His disciples and shows his deepest desires and directions for all of his children, followers, believers, and non-believers by giving twenty-six (26) Characteristics on Christian Leadership. Study carefully verses 1-6 as referenced in this manual. (Verses 7- 26 should be studied at home or church bible study. Christian Leadership is your Discipleship.)

> **Your willingness to serve in your church and community, beyond the gates, is an outward demonstration of your spiritual maturity as an obedient and disciplined follower of Christ Jesus.**

GOD'S PLAN FOR AN ABUNDANT LIFE: Stewardship, Tithing & Discipleship

What Is Discipleship?

A Disciple: May be defined as a learned person who believes in the Teaching and Training of a given philosophy and/or theology; to learn and become disciplined to a teaching as a way of life. As a disciple of Jesus, to comprehend and to Understand — to Accept – and believe in this way of life:

1. a pupil or follower of any teacher or school of religion, learning, art, etc.
2. an early follower of Jesus, esp. one of the Apostles
3. a member of the Disciples of Christ
4. SYN. FOLLOWER discipleship n.

Disciple implies a personal, devoted relationship to the teacher of some doctrine or leader of some movement [Plato was a disciple of Socrates]; partisan, in this connection, refers to an unswerving, often blindly devoted, adherent of some person or cause (Webster Dictionary)

Discipline:

1. a branch of knowledge or learning

2. a) training that develops self-control, character, or orderliness and efficiency
   b) strict control to enforce obedience

3. the result of such training or control; specif.,
   a) self-control or orderly conduct
   b) acceptance of or submission to authority and control

4. a system of rules, as for a church or monastic order

5. treatment that corrects or punishes, to subject to discipline; train; control

SYN. follower is the general term for one who follows or believes in the teachings or theories of someone

> This act of leadership is called **Discipleship**, drawing the unsaved and saved into a new or closer relationship with Christ.
>
> **Discipleship** is the winning of hearts and souls to Christ.

GOD'S PLAN FOR AN ABUNDANT LIFE: Stewardship, Tithing & Discipleship

What is Discipleship?

- Discipleship is an act of the Disciple, a willing humble servant, who has given their heart, mind and soul to God and is so Christ-centered that others will marvel at the anointing, power, and the authority of Christ in their life. In other words people will see Christ in you and even your enemies will come to know you as Blessed Men and Women of God.

- Everything that a Disciple does is based on love and one's reasonable service to glorify God.

Let Him that is Greater in you fight your battles, for we can do all things through Christ who strengthens us.

- The whole understanding of Discipleship and Leadership is predicated on accepting that God is the creator and owner of everything. **<u>Everything you have belongs to God.</u>**

- You are a Steward of the manifold Blessings that God has given to you and the privilege to experience the abundance of his riches in glory, II Corth. 4:17. Only God knows your future, he has already predestinated our lives. However, he has given you free will through your mind to make decisions.

Wherever your destiny is, your present state of mind is not sufficient to get you there. You must Fellowship with Christ to Establish a New and Closer Relationship with Christ. Let your mind be in Christ Jesus, Phil. 2:5, and your fleshly and lustful ways will die, but you must submit to His Will and Not Your Will. In Jeremiah 29:11 God says " For I know the plans I have for you," declares the Lord, "plans to prosper you and not to harm you, plans to give you hope and a future".

- "Greater is He that is in you, than he that is in the world". Allow Him, who created you, to release your prosperity and the abundant treasures laid up for you in His Storehouse (church), for such a Season of Harvest.

    1 John 4:4 *Ye are of God, little children, and have overcome them: because greater is he that is in you, than he that is in the world.*

- Disciples know that their breakthroughs, victories, refreshing, anointing, and triumphs over every situation only come when they operate in the wisdom of God. Let Him that is Greater in you fight your battles, for we can do all things through Christ who strengthens us.

GOD'S PLAN FOR AN ABUNDANT LIFE: Stewardship, Tithing & Discipleship

What is Discipleship?

Disciples understand God's Majesty, Dominion, Power, His Greatness, and Lordship. By His Divine Revelations they are Given Knowledge to run and do what Jesus has called them to do.

- In **Isaiah 40:31** the word says, *"But they that wait upon the Lord shall renew their strength; they shall mount up with wings as eagles;* **they shall run***, and* **not be weary; and they shall walk, and not faint.***"*

Disciples have learned that they can not trust their thinking to establish or to accomplish what they are charged to do. Actually, the mind absent of the Holy Spirit is not capable of handling what God has called you to do. You must become new creatures in Christ Jesus, and the old things will pass away. "The Paradigm Shift", is moving you from how you used to think, as a carnal minded, powerless person satisfied with just enough, to a spiritually disciplined and obedient God-centered person that is as a doer of the Word.

They maximize every moment in their lives for the Glory of God, and they expect the abundant blessings of God. Jesus taught us in John 10:10 that *"The thief cometh not, but for to steal, and to kill, and to destroy:* **I am come that they might have life, and that they might have it more abundantly.***"*

> **"The Paradigm Shift"**, is moving you from how you used to think, as a carnal minded, powerless person satisfied with just enough, to a spiritually disciplined and obedient God-centered person that is as a doer of the Word.

- God does not just Bless you in the physical realm. He also, blesses you spiritually, through the redemptive Blood of His Son. He who died for us paid a price and took upon Himself the chastisement for our sins.

- Yet, by His Grace and Mercy, listen to what Paul has learned and teaches us about Jesus:

    III John 1:2 *"Beloved, I wish above all things that thou mayest prosper and be in health, even as thy soul prospereth"*.

Your health is the physical and natural domains of life. The spirit deals with the condition of your mind and your soul.

The devil and the forces of evil and darkness are in constant battle with your state of mind. It is a battle between the Flesh and the Holy Spirit. That's why you must know who the enemy is and how to dress for spiritual warfare.

GOD'S PLAN FOR AN ABUNDANT LIFE: Stewardship, Tithing & Discipleship

What is Discipleship?

Disciples Put On The Whole Armor of God

Ephesians 6:10-18 *Finally, my brethren, be strong in the Lord, and in the power of his might. [11] Put on the whole armour of God, that ye may be able to stand against the wiles of the devil. [12] For we wrestle not against flesh and blood, but against principalities, against powers, against the rulers of the darkness of this world, against spiritual wickedness in high places. [13] Wherefore take unto you the whole armour of God, that ye may be able to withstand in the evil day, and having done all, to stand. [14] Stand therefore, having your loins girt about with truth, and having on the breastplate of righteousness;*

[15] And your feet shod with the preparation of the gospel of peace; [16] Above all, taking the shield of faith, wherewith ye shall be able to quench all the fiery darts of the wicked. [17] And take the helmet of salvation, and the sword of the Spirit, which is the word of God: [18] Praying always with all prayer and supplication in the Spirit, and watching thereunto with all perseverance and supplication for all saints;

Disciples Are In The World But Not of The World

As Disciples, you must come out of the world and into the heavenly places of Christ Jesus. Disciples know that their journey here on earth first requires that they have heavenly experiences in the earth.

Matthew 6:10-11 tells us, *"Thy kingdom come. Thy will be done **in earth**, as it is **in heaven**. Give us this day our daily bread."*

These powerful scriptures are the principal foundations of your power base. You must meditate on the things of God. This is confirmed in:

Joshua 1:8 *"This book of the law shall not depart out of thy mouth; but thou shalt meditate therein day and night, that thou mayest observe to do according to all that is written therein: for then thou shalt make thy way prosperous, and then thou shalt have good success".*

Disciples Think On These Things:

Philip. 4:8 *Finally, brethren, whatsoever things are true, whatsoever things are honest, whatsoever things are just, whatsoever things are pure, whatsoever things are lovely, whatsoever things are of good report; if there be any virtue, and if there be any praise, think on these things.*

GOD'S PLAN FOR AN ABUNDANT LIFE: Stewardship, Tithing & Discipleship

What is Discipleship?

Philip. 4:19 *But my God shall supply all your need **according to his riches in glory by Christ Jesus**.*

Galatians 6:3 *For if a man think himself to be something, when he is nothing, he deceiveth himself.*

Ephs. 3:20 *Now unto him that is able to do exceeding abundantly above all that we ask or think, according to the power that worketh in us,*

As a Disciple you must come to know that you are to be a modern day Paul. The Lord instructs you in Matthew 28:18-20 that because He has all power in His hand you can go and make Disciples. He has given you the Power. He backs up this statement by saying in **Matthew 28:20 "Teaching them to observe all things whatsoever I have commanded you: and, lo, I am with you always, even unto the end of the world. Amen".** In other words if you do God's Will, you will never be alone. He will always provide and make a way for you. He will come to you, and reveal His presence and Glory to and through you when you continue to draw near to Him. Leaders who serve and accept the mantel of Discipleship (Christian Leaders) know that in all their getting, get understanding: Read the following scriptures:

Proverbs 4:7 says, *"Wisdom is the principal thing; therefore get wisdom: and with all thy getting get understanding."*

Proverbs 3:5 *"Trust in the Lord with all thine heart; and lean not unto thine own understanding."*

Eccles. 7:12 *"For wisdom is a defence, and money is a defence: but the excellency of knowledge is, that wisdom giveth life to them that have it."*

Eccles. 10:19 *A feast is made for laughter, and wine maketh merry: but money answereth all things.*

We must reverence the Holiness of God, for we have learned in Proverbs 1:7 that **"The fear of the Lord is the beginning of knowledge: but fools despise wisdom and instruction, for the Lord giveth wisdom: out of his mouth cometh knowledge and understanding,** Proverbs 2:6".

GOD'S PLAN FOR AN ABUNDANT LIFE: Stewardship, Tithing & Discipleship

Paradigm Shift

Disciples Must Have A "Paradigm Shift" In Their Thinking and Understanding of:

- How You Think, and What You Meditate On/About?

- Whose You Are and Who You Are?

- What Is Your Present Condition and Your Future Position?

- What Are Your Weaknesses and Strengths?

- Why You Do What You Do and for Who?

- Your Lack and Your Abundance

- God's Gifts to You and Your Anointing

- Using The Anointing, Power and Authority

- Activating Your Faith and Realizing Your Abundance

- The Ways of God and His Love for You

I. Group Exercise on Discipleship Principles:

Instructions:
- Table Groups: Team up in groups
- Read scriptures, each team will read, select key verses, and highlight key words
- Summarize Team Group selections with brief comments
- Group Summarize your Final Selections and Record
- Document group responses and post up with tape or pin up on wall(s)

GOD'S PLAN FOR AN ABUNDANT LIFE: Stewardship, Tithing & Discipleship

Discipleship Principles

Complete by filling in the blanks from the scripture verses below.

Prov 3:1-10

In verse 1 & 2; Solomon says "if we let thine heart keep my commandments we shall be rewarded with 3 things: _____ _____ _____.
What are the 3 blessing for these two commands?

In verse 3 & 4; Let not mercy and truth forsake thee: What shall we bind about our neck _____ and write then upon the _____ of _____ _____. And thou shall find _____ and _____ _____ in the sight of _____ and _____.

> **Luke 6:38** *Give, and it shall be given unto you; good measure, pressed down, and shaken together, and running over, shall men give into your bosom. For with the same measure that ye mete withal it shall be measured to you again.*

In verse 5 & 6; Who shall we trust in _____ _____ with all thine _____ and _____ not to _____ own _____? How shall we acknowledge God: _____ _____ _____ _____. And He shall _____ thy _____.

Be not wise in thine own eyes and fear the _____ and depart from what? _____. What will God bless you with if you depart from _____. You shall receive _____ to your _____ and _____ to thy _____.

In verse 9 & 10; Solomon says "that we shall _____ the _____ with the _____ of all thine _____. When we honor God what will happen? (So shall thy _____ be _____ with _____ and thy _____ shall _____ _____ with new _____.

123

Copyright © 2002 VASTT Ministry & Publishing

GOD'S PLAN FOR AN ABUNDANT LIFE: Stewardship, Tithing & Discipleship

Discipleship Principles

I. Instructions: Group Exercise on Discipleship Principles:

- **GROUPS:** Team up in equal groups (please, with people you do not know, have a biblical based person per group if possible)

- Group size determined by diving number of participants in equal groups

- Each team will read Proverb 3:1-10, and discuss each scripture and answer questions as a group response, (select spokes person)

- Also select key Power verses, and highlight power words

- Summarize Team selections with brief comments, select presenter

- Group Summarize your Final Selections and document group responses

- Post easel paper up with tape or pin up on wall

Identify what you feel are major points in the following scripture verses.

> **Proverbs 3:1-10** *My son, forget not my law; but let thine heart keep my commandments: [2] For length of days, and long life, and peace, shall they add to thee.*
>
> *[3] Let not mercy and truth forsake thee: bind them about thy neck; write them upon the table of thine heart: [4] So shalt thou find favour and good understanding in the sight of God and man.*
>
> *[5] Trust in the Lord with all thine heart; and lean not unto thine own understanding. [6] In all thy ways acknowledge him, and he shall direct thy paths.*
>
> *[7] Be not wise in thine own eyes: fear the Lord, and depart from evil. [8] It shall be health to thy navel, and marrow to thy bones.*
>
> *[9] Honour the Lord with thy substance, and with the firstfruits of all thine increase: [10] So shall thy barns be filled with plenty, and thy presses shall burst out with new wine.*

Discipleship Principles

II. Treasure Chest of Knowledge.

In this group exercise see if you can find the keys that will unlock your Treasure Chest. The Abundance of Life is locked inside of you. This section will focus on John 17:1-26. John gives twenty-six Leadership Characteristics of a Disciple. There is power from the anointing in each verse.

> **Paul said in 2 Cor. 4:7**, *"that we have this treasure in earthly vessels that the Excellency of the Power may be of God and not us. Discipline your minds to focus on the spirit."*

The transformation of the mind begins with what you think and believe. You have been given power through Christ Jesus. Lean not to thine own understanding but in all thy ways acknowledge Him and He shall direct thy path.

1. Depending on the size of the group the scripture verses will be assigned to each table
2. Study assigned scriptures John 17:1-6
3. Identify and list the Characteristic in each verse
4. Be creative and develop a way to demonstrate the characteristics in this seminar
5. You may use other references to give additional emphasis
6. Identify a characteristic you feel you need to grow in

Read, take notes and share thoughts with each other:

> **John 17:1-6** *These words spake Jesus, and lifted up his eyes to heaven, and said, Father, the hour is come; glorify thy Son, that thy Son also may glorify thee: [2] As thou hast given him power over all flesh, that he should give eternal life to as many as thou hast given him. [3] And this is life eternal, that they might know thee the only true God, and Jesus Christ, whom thou hast sent. [4] I have glorified thee on the earth: I have finished the work which thou gavest me to do. [5] And now, O Father, glorify thou me with thine own self with the glory which I had with thee before the world was. [6] I have manifested thy name unto the men which thou gavest me out of the world: thine they were, and thou gavest them me; and they have kept thy word.*

GOD'S PLAN FOR AN ABUNDANT LIFE: Stewardship, Tithing & Discipleship

Christian Discipleship & Leadership Characteristics

V1. Disciples Lift Up The Name of Jesus.

Disciples to can draw all men unto them when they glorify the ways and works of the Word of God through Christ Jesus

> **John 12:32-33** *(32) And I, if I be lifted up from the earth, will draw all men unto me. [33] This he said, signifying what death he should die.*

They Glorify God:

They magnify God through praising His name and honoring His commandments (Ps. 86:11-13). Jesus also glorified His father through His perfect obedience and His sacrificial death on our behalf.

> **Psalm 86:11-13** *Teach me thy way, O Lord; I will walk in thy truth: unite my heart to fear thy name. [12] I will praise thee, O Lord my God, with all my heart: and I will glorify thy name for evermore. [13] For great is thy mercy toward me: and thou hast delivered my soul from the lowest hell. [KJV]*

They Demonstrate An Out Pouring of Love.

> **John 13:34-35** *A new commandment I give unto you, That ye love one another; as I have loved you, that ye also love one another. [35] By this shall all men know that ye are my disciples, if ye have love one to another.*

V2. Disciples have been given <u>Power and Authority</u> to overcome their fleshly desires. They are able to operate in the anointing of their gifts.

> **Galatians 5:18-22** *But if ye be led of the Spirit, ye are not under the law. [19] Now the works of the flesh are manifest, which are these; Adultery, fornication, uncleanness, lasciviousness, [20] Idolatry, witchcraft, hatred, variance, emulations, wrath, strife, seditions, heresies, [21] Envyings, murders, drunkenness, revellings, and such like: of the which I tell you before, as I have also told you in time past, that they which do such things shall not inherit the kingdom of God.*

They operate in the Fruit of the Spirit.

There are visible signs in their daily behavior and mannerisms. They exemplify *"the fruit of the Spirit in love, joy, peace, longsuffering, gentleness, goodness, faith, Gal 5:22 [KJV]*

GOD'S PLAN FOR AN ABUNDANT LIFE: Stewardship, Tithing & Discipleship

Christian Discipleship & Leadership Characteristics

V3. Disciples have New Life (Eternal Life) and They Know Jesus. They live their lives according to the Word of God.

They Know Jesus and are Saved

1 John 5:12-15 *He that hath the Son hath life; and he that hath not the Son of God hath not life. [13] These things have I written unto you that believe on the name of the Son of God; that ye may know that ye have eternal life, and that ye may believe on the name of the Son of God. [14] And this is the confidence that we have in him, that, if we ask any thing according to his will, he heareth us: [15] And if we know that he hear us, whatsoever we ask, we know that we have the petitions that we desired of him. [KJV]*

Romans 10:9 *That if thou shalt confess with thy mouth the Lord Jesus, and shalt believe in thine heart that God hath raised him from the dead, thou shalt be saved. [KJV]*

Romans 10:13 *For whosoever shall call upon the name of the Lord shall be saved. [KJV]*

> **Eternal Life —**
> a person's new and redeemed existence in Jesus Christ that is granted by God as a gift to all believers. Eternal life refers to the quality or character of our new existence in Christ as well as the unending character of that life.

V4. Disciples Finish The Work and are Blessed By God In All That They Do. They have the ability to work well with others and to help others in accomplishing their work.

Isaiah 50:4 *The Lord God hath given me the tongue of the learned, that I should know how to speak a word in season to him that is weary: he wakeneth morning by morning, he wakeneth mine ear to hear as the learned. [KJV]*

Matthew 25:35 *For I was an hungered, and ye gave me meat: I was thirsty, and ye gave me drink: I was a stranger, and ye took me in:*

Christian Discipleship & Leadership Characteristics

V5. Disciples Know God As The Alpha and The Omega, The Creator of the Universe.

Isaiah 40:28 *Do you not know? Have you not heard? The Lord is the everlasting God, the Creator of the ends of the earth. He will not grow tired or weary, and his understanding no one can fathom.* [NIV]

Isaiah 43:15 *I am the Lord, your Holy One, Israel's Creator, your King."* [NIV]

Rev. 1:8 *I am Alpha and Omega, the beginning and the ending, saith the Lord, which is, and which was, and which is to come, the Almighty.* [KJV]

Rev. 21:6 *And he said unto me, It is done. I am Alpha and Omega, the beginning and the end. I will give unto him that is athirst of the fountain of the water of life freely.* [KJV]

Rev. 22:13 *I am Alpha and Omega, the beginning and the end, the first and the last.* [KJV]

V6. Disciples Teach and Live According To The Word of Jesus.

Acts 20:32 *And now, brethren, I commend you to God, and to the word of his grace, which is able to build you up, and to give you an inheritance among all them which are sanctified.* [KJV

Matthew 4:4 *But he answered and said, It is written, Man shall not live by bread alone, but by every word that proceedeth out of the mouth of God.* [KJV]

Deut. 8:3 *And he humbled thee, and suffered thee to hunger, and fed thee with manna, which thou knewest not, neither did thy fathers know; that he might make thee know that man doth not live by bread only, but by every word that proceedeth out of the mouth of the Lord doth man live.* [KJV]

1 Tim. 4:6 *If thou put the brethren in remembrance of these things, thou shalt be a good minister of Jesus Christ, nourished up in the words of faith and of good doctrine, whereunto thou hast attained.* [KJV]

Christian Discipleship & Leadership Characteristics

GOD'S PLAN FOR AN ABUNDANT LIFE: Stewardship, Tithing & Discipleship

V7. They Know All Things Come From God.

V8. They Know and Believe in the Word of God.

V9. They Pray and Believe In The Power of Prayer and They Pray for Others.

V10. They Are Children of God and Believe That We Are All Children of God.

V11. They Are Transformed By the Renewing of Their Minds, and Will Lead Others to Christ;

V12. They Watch-Over Others, Keeping Them from Straying Away From God's Commandments.

V13. They Have Joy In Their Lives, and Are Fruitful.

V14. They Have Been Persecuted for The Name of Jesus and His Righteousness.

V15. They Pray for Salvation of Others

V16. They Are Not of This World.

V17. They have Been Sanctified and Know The Word Is Truth.

V18. They Are Sent To Do God's Work and They Know that God Has A Plan for them.

V19. They Lead Others To Salvation through Christ

V20. They Pray for People To Become Believers and Come To Know the Word of God.

V21. They Believe In The Unity and Body of Christ, and Operate In Spirit of One Accord.

V22. They Are Humble Servants and Glorify God In Their Daily Lives.

V23. They Know That Jesus Gave His Life; they are Re-deemed By The Shedding of His Blood. They Know There Is No Other Love Greater Than That of God.

V21. They Believe In The Unity and Body of Christ, and Operate In Spirit of One Accord.

V22. They Are Humble Servants and Glorify God In Their Daily Lives.

V23. They Know That Jesus Gave His Life; they are Re-deemed By The Shedding of His Blood. They Know There Is No Other Love Greater Than That of Our Father God.

V24. They Desire Others To Come To Know God, Who Loved Them Even In The Belly of Their Mothers Womb, Even Before Time.

V25. They Know God To Be Righteous In Spite of The World Not Following Christ.

V26. They Spread the Name of Jesus. They Desire Others To Know The Love God Has for Them.

Copyright © 2002 VASTI Ministry & Publishing

GOD'S PLAN FOR AN ABUNDANT LIFE: Stewardship, Tithing & Discipleship

Christian Discipleship & Leadership Characteristics

How do you demonstrate your understanding of the following scripture? Disciples are Believers who accept the greatest commandment given when Jesus said:

III. Disciples Love the Lord, & Their Neighbors

MATTHEW 22:36-40 *Master, **which is the great commandment in the law?** [37] Jesus said unto him, Thou shalt love the Lord thy God with all thy heart, and with all thy soul, and with all thy mind. [38] This is the first and great commandment. [39] And the second is like unto it, Thou shalt love thy neighbour as thyself. [40] On these two commandments hang all the law and the prophets.* KJV

Discuss the following question related to Matthew 22:36-40

If you really love Jesus can you live by the above commandments?

_____
_____
_____
_____
_____
_____

Why do you think people have a problem living up to this scripture?

_____
_____
_____
_____
_____
_____

Christian Discipleship & Leadership Characteristics

Do these exercise make you question or at least re-think your relationship with Jesus? Explain.

_____
_____
_____
_____
_____
_____

You can not be an effective disciple, nor a church leader, when you refuse to live according to the Word of God. Right now the Lord is telling you to surrender totally to Him. Would you agree or disagree? Explain.

_____
_____
_____
_____
_____
_____
_____
_____
_____
_____
_____
_____
_____

Christian Discipleship & Leadership Characteristics

IV. Disciples Are Made Not Born.

In Matthew 28:18-20 You Will Note hat Jesus Says: Matthew 28:18

And Jesus came and spake unto them, saying, all _____ is given unto me in _____. V19 _____ ye therefore, and _____ (NASB says make disciples) all nations, baptizing them in the name of the Father, and of the Son, and of the Holy Ghost: V20. _____ them to observe all things whatsoever I have commanded you: and, _____ (knows) I am with you even unto the _____ of the world. Amen.

V. Study and Know The Truth

As you will come to know, a Disciple is taught, receives and follows instruction. These instructions come from the Lord Himself, and are available in you. In view of this understanding we must also acknowledge that if one is to be taught then the student/disciple must Study. Paul, writes in: **2 Tim. 2:15:**

_____ to shew thyself _____ unto God, a_____ that needeth not to be _____, _____ dividing the word of _____.

For the sake of this training the word Leadership is synonymous with Discipleship and has a strong correlation with Ministry and even Shepherd. As we look at these titles there is a common thread linking them together. Regardless to the title, each must have a Christ Centered Attitude and have Christ Likeness. The life of Jesus exemplifies the servant attitude and humility. With all power in His hand, He allowed Himself to take on the iniquity of our sin-sick souls. He demonstrated his obedience to God by being a faithful Servant. He washes the feet of those he called and taught as disciples.

John 13:5

After that he poureth water into a bason, and began to _____ the _____ _____ and to wipe them with the towel wherewith he was girded.

Christian Discipleship & Leadership Characteristics

John 13:14 *If I then, your Lord and Master, have washed your feet; ye also ought to wash one another's feet.*

1 Peter 5:6

_____ yourselves therefore under the mighty hand of _____, that he may _____ you in due time:

Paul teaches us that we must become servants of the gospel, which is given as a gift by the Grace of God through the working of His Power.

Ephes. 3:7 *I became a servant of this gospel by the gift of God's grace given me through the working of his power.*

VI. Prerequisites For Becoming A Disciple:

1. **Belief that Jesus Died and Rose From The Dead To Save You**

    Romans 10:9 That if thou shalt _____ with thy _____ the Lord Jesus, and shalt _____ in thine _____ that God hath _____ him from the _____, thou shalt be _____.

2. **Follows Jesus**

    Matthew 16:24-25 24 Then _____ Jesus unto his _____, If any man will _____after me, let him ____himself, and _____ ___ ___ _____, and follow me. 25 For _____ will _____ his life shall _____ ____: and whosoever will _____ his life for my _____shall find it.

3. **Have Faith**

    Hebrews 11:1 ____ _____ is the _____ of things _____ for, the _____ of things not _____.

GOD'S PLAN FOR AN ABUNDANT LIFE: Stewardship, Tithing & Discipleship

Christian Discipleship & Leadership Characteristics

4. **Is Born Again (John 3:7). Becomes A New Creature, and Has Been Transformed By The Renewing of Your Mind. (Ro. 12:2)**

   2 Cor. 5:17 Therefore if any ____ be in Christ, he is a new _____: old things are _____ away; behold, all _____ are become new.

   Romans 12:2 And be not conformed to this world: but be ye _____ by the _____ of your _____, that ye may _____ what is that _____, and _____, and _____, will of God.

5. **Seeks A Life That Glorifies God**

   Matthew 6:33 But _____ ye first the _____ of God, and his _____; and all these _____ shall be _____ unto you.

6. **Trust in God and Self Denial (Flesh and Lust)**

   Romans 7:18 For I _____ that in ____ (that is, in my flesh,) dwelleth no _____ thing: for to _____ ___ _____ with me; but how to _____ that which is _____ I find not.

7. **Lives What He Teaches (Christ Like Attitude)**
   1 Cor. 9:26-27 _____ I do not ___ like a man running _____; I do not _____ like a man _____ the air. No, I _____ my body and make it my _____ so that after I have _____ to _____, I myself will not be _____ for the _____. NIV

8. **Lead Others To Christ (Evangelist)**

   John 17:19 For _____ _____ _____ myself, that they too may be truly _____.

134

Christian Discipleship & Leadership Characteristics

9. **Disciples Have Power to Teach**

    Acts 1:8 But ye shall receive power, after that the Holy Ghost is come upon you: and ye shall be witnesses unto me both in Jerusalem, and in all Judaea, and in Samaria, and unto the uttermost part of the earth.   KJV

10. **Has A Servant's Heart and Is A Good Steward**

    Mark 9:35 And he ____ down, and _____ the _____, and saith unto them, If any ____ desire to be _____, the _____ shall be _____ of all, and _____ of all. KJV

    Matthew 23:11-12 But he that is _____ among you shall be your _____. And _____ shall _____ himself shall be _____; and he that shall _____ himself shall be _____.

    Notes: _____
    _____
    _____
    _____
    _____
    _____
    _____
    _____
    _____

GOD'S PLAN FOR AN ABUNDANT LIFE: Stewardship, Tithing & Discipleship

A Church Case Study

Discipleship Group Exercise

I. A Briefing for the Case Study:

There are issues, problems and concerns that are plaguing the growth of the church and the broader community. There is a recession in the land. People are in need of food, jobs, job training, clothing, housing, daycare, health care, and counseling services, just to name a few. There is a growing population of seniors and in the next 10 to 20 years there will be a tremendous need for new levels of human services for this population. The church is composed of more adults and young adults with families, female single-head of household, and a good number of mature religious folks and mature Christians. The average income is between $12 to $35 thousand dollars per year. Hidden in many of the church families are significant others who are not active members nor involved with supporting the church. However, they are being Blessed by the Grace and Mercy of God because of the person in their life who is trying to grow closer, trust more, and depend more on the Lord. In many cases it is the male who is absent from his position of authority in the House of God that plagues our families.

> **Hidden in many of the church families are significant others who are not active members nor involved with supporting the church.**

Marriages, families and communities are being destroyed by divorce. Unemployment, health issues, lack of care services, low wages, sex, drugs, guns, anger, and violence along with financial stress is affecting the very stability God has planned for the family. We must turn back to Jesus and use the power of God to stump and smite satan and the forces of evil.

The youth in the church and in the broader community do not understand the power that is within them and they are so rebellious. Many are from single homes and have so much idle time they do not know of their creative abilities or the gifts that rest within each of them. Drugs and gangs are ever prevalent problems and the youth feel no one really hears their cries. Teen pregnancy and suicide have reached alarming levels in minority communities. Talented, gifted youth have limited education and culturally enriched programs that once existed in their communities, are now gone.

The Pastor, called by God, and fully anointed, has heard from God time and time again. He [has seen] the Visions from God that will make the church and its members free of debt. He believes Christ will reveal Himself to the church body. God has given him continuous proclamation and revelation to bring the Vision into full manifestation. Every gift seen and unseen is or will be available saith the Lord to the Pastor.

136

GOD'S PLAN FOR AN ABUNDANT LIFE: Stewardship, Tithing & Discipleship

A Church Case Study

Discipleship Group Exercise

The Pastor wants to build and expand the church and the level of ministries through the church, to meet the needs of the community and church families. He has shared the Visions with the leaders/disciples/ministers of the church. The Pastor's concern for the well-being of the church family and those of the broader community will now be discussed.

God has called your Pastor to launch out into the deep and trust Him for the end results. *In His vision from God there are revelation, that the church, its leadership and members will have some of the following experiences:*

- A Higher level in Praise and Worship Service
- Tremendous increase in Tithes and Offerings
- The entire Body of Christ being on one accord
- Miracles, Signs and Wonders
- A Breakthrough in ministries and personal endeavors
- An Increase in membership
- Overflow of Laborers to meet the needs of the people
- An Explosion of Entrepreneurs associated with and through the church will meet every need of the Church and community
- Increase in ministerial staff, elders, deacons leaders of outreach ministries.
- Marriages saved
- Number of teen pregnancy dropped
- Gang violence irradicated. (Stopping the killing of our youth.)

Please know that many talents and abundant gifts yet to be revealed, lie dormant in too many churches. The Pastor has scheduled on-going training workshops and seminars to help the church grow in their fellowship and relationship with Christ. The only concern is that the Pastor can not do this by himself.

As Disciples and or leaders of the church you have been assembled and told that only through your combined efforts, commitments, and obedience will the Vision become a reality. He has organized a Stewardship Ministry to implement God's Vision, and you have been Chosen.

GOD'S PLAN FOR AN ABUNDANT LIFE: Stewardship, Tithing & Discipleship

A Church Case Study

Discipleship Group Exercise

II. Your Group Challenge:

A. Discuss with your group how you as the Disciples for Christ will lead other church members to meet the challenge of making God's Vision to the Pastor a reality.

B. You are ambassadors for Christ, giving witness to what thus said the Lord. You are to help lead your Church and your families to become willing vessels of God.

C. How will you lead and teach the congregation to believe that they can do all things through Christ Jesus? Remember what Paul teaches in Philippians. (Read)

> **Philip. 4:5-7,** *"Let your moderation be known unto all men". The Lord is at hand. Be careful for nothing; but in every thing by prayer and supplication with thanksgiving let your requests be made known unto God. And the peace of God,* **which passeth all understanding, shall keep your hearts and minds through Christ Jesus".**

> **Philip. 4:19** *And know* **"But my God shall supply all your needs according to his riches in glory by Christ Jesus.**

III. Your Mission:

1. Accept the Mantle of God's Calling on your life to support the Ministry of your church. You are not here by accident.

   a. John 15:15-17 *Henceforth I call you not servants; for the servant knoweth not what his lord doeth: but I have called you friends; for all things that I have heard of my Father I have made known unto you. [16] Ye have not chosen me, but I have chosen you, and ordained you, that ye should go and bring forth fruit, and that your fruit should remain: that whatsoever ye shall ask of the Father in my name, he may give it you. [17] These things I command you, that ye love one another.*

2. Accept the Pastor's Vision and Trust God for the Victory

3. Accept a position of Leadership to support the church's Stewardship Journey

GOD'S PLAN FOR AN ABUNDANT LIFE: Stewardship, Tithing & Discipleship

A Church Case Study

Discipleship Group Exercise

4. Work with your team ministry (table group) and collectively listen and share

5. Identify ways, through ideas and examples, that you feel will lead the entire church to give their Tithes and Give their Offerings: Develop a list of power words and power scriptures.

6. Humble yourself and learn to trust others and know that you can not lead if you can not follow directions

7. Develop a Plan of Action that the majority of your group feels will help the church reach its goals and objectives

8. List the goals and objectives for your plan of action.

9. What is your responsibility and commitment to the journey?
    a. List your commitments and those of your team
    b. Will you pay your tithes and give your offerings according to God's Word?
    c. How will you give of your time, talents and treasures? Give examples that can be shared with the congregation.

10. What Biblical stories will you use to share with others?
    a. List five to seven stories from your team
    b. Which two biblical stories (make it personal) can you relate to, and will this help the church reach its Visions?

11. Which scriptures had an impact on you and the team?
    a. List five to seven scriptures from your team and Why?
    b. Identify and list at least two of your favorite scriptures

12. How would you improve on becoming a better church leader and when will you begin to live up to what you are saying?

Your group may decide to add more items to the above list of twelve. Please note that your attitude and the Words that you speak concerning this training will either convict you even more, or you will continue to find excuses and dilute the power of God locked up in you. The Power is in your Words.

GOD'S PLAN FOR AN ABUNDANT LIFE: Stewardship, Tithing & Discipleship

A Church Case Study
Discipleship Group Exercise

Remember that the Holy Spirit is working in the Power of believers. This task is not hard.

- **Select key Words and verses (power words and power scriptures.)**

- **Split the work up in groups**

- **Select scriptures you have read during the training session, from previous readings and what the Lord reveals through each of you.**

- **All the answers will be compiled and given back to your Pastor, the Stewardship Director for future review and trainings.**

We hope that this exercise training will be viewed as an outward expression that you indeed have experienced an inward spiritual transformation/Paradigm Shift. It is a move away from what you used to do, to a more excellent example, as in **Daniel 6:3,** *"Then this Daniel was preferred above the presidents and princes, because an excellent spirit was in him; and the king thought to set him over the whole realm."*

GOD'S PLAN FOR AN ABUNDANT LIFE: Stewardship, Tithing & Discipleship

A Church Case Study

Discipleship Group Exercise

IV. Instructions:

Read the following scripture verses on III John 1:1-12 on the next page. In this exercise create and/or expand on your Scripture and Power Word List. Select the best scriptures and Power Words. Summarize the existing list. All the information shared will be compiled and later used to help promote the Stewardship Journey.

The facilitator's words of encouragement are inspired by the Holy Spirit. " May the Lord continuously richly Bless you, the Pastor, the flock and His Disciples."

No Greater Joy Than Knowing The Truth

3 John 1:1-12 *The elder unto the well beloved Gaius, whom I love in the truth. 2Beloved, I wish above all things that thou mayest prosper and be in health, even as thy soul prospereth. 3For I rejoiced greatly, when the brethren came and testified of the truth that is in thee, even as thou walkest in the truth. 4I have no greater joy than to hear that my children walk in truth. 5Beloved, thou doest faithfully whatsoever thou doest to the brethren, and to strangers; 6Which have borne witness of thy charity before the church: whom if thou bring 4forward on their journey after a godly sort, thou shalt do well: 7Because that for his name's sake they went forth, taking nothing of the Gentiles. 8We therefore ought to receive such, that we might be fellow helpers to the truth. 9I wrote unto the church: but Diotrephes, who loveth to have the preeminence among them, receiveth us not. 10Wherefore, if I come, I will remember his deeds which he doeth, prating against us with malicious words: and not content therewith, neither doth he himself receive the brethren, and forbiddeth them that would, and casteth them out of the church. 11Beloved, follow not that which is evil, but that which is good. He that doeth good is of God: but he that doeth evil hath not seen God. 12Demetrius hath good report of all men, and of the truth itself: yea, and we also bear record; and ye know that our record is true.*

_____
_____
_____
_____
_____
_____

Copyright © 2002 VASTT Ministry & Publishing

GOD'S PLAN FOR AN ABUNDANT LIFE: Stewardship, Tithing & Discipleship

12 Principles of Discipleship

1. Salvation: Grace and Mercy

2. Prayer and Fasting, Praise, and Worship

3. Give Your Tithes and Offerings

4. Seek Ye First The Kingdom

5. Put On The Whole Armour of God

6. Walk In The Fruit of The Spirit

7. Keep Your Mind Stayed on Jesus

8. Ask, Seek and Knock

9. Be Ye Transformed By the Renewing of Your Mind

10. Walk In Faith and Let Your Light Shine

11. We Are Children of God, Then Heirs To The Kingdom of God

12. The Anointing, The Power and The Authority

GOD'S PLAN FOR AN ABUNDANT LIFE: Stewardship, Tithing & Discipleship

Study Sheets

Stewardship Characteristics

A Life of Discipleship & Stewardship = 100% Tither

Servants Then Heirs

Committed To God

Serving With A Willing Heart

Acknowledges:

Every Good and Perfect Gift Comes From God

Become A Kingdom Builder

Experience Heaven On Earth

Spread The Gospel of Jesus

Giving and Living According To God's Plan

Become a New Creature In Christ Jesus

Notes